PA Guide to
Going Digital

Linda Bennett

THE **PUBLISHERS**
ASSOCIATION

Published by:
The Publishers Association
29B Montague Street
London
WC1B 5BW
t +44 (0)207 691 9191
f +44(0) 207 691 9199
e mail@publishers.org.uk
w www.publishers.org.uk

ISBN: 978-0-85386-344-1

Front cover graphic: (c) Amanda Hawkes
Graphics of E-readers from manufacturers
All other graphics unless otherwise indicated, sourced from Fotolia.com
Printed and bound in the UK by Lightning Source UK Ltd, Milton Keynes, Buckinghamshire

Contents

Part Two | Opportunities

Tables

Figures

Foreword

It's happening, quickly now. Journals are 90 per cent of the way there; the academic library market for e-books is fast maturing; e-textbooks await only a viable business model; and consumer e-book players are making their moves. Digital delivery is now an essential skill set for most publishers. The opportunities are there, but the choices to be made and the issues to be confronted can be daunting.

This report is part manual, part reference, part directory. It offers a rapid tour of the field for the unengaged or uninitiated, but it also offers a useful overview and update of the technical options available and the issues that a digital publisher must address in deciding on format and channel to market for those needing to reappraise their offer.

It surveys the current status of market opportunities internationally, and includes useful contact information for purchasing consortia and potential suppliers.

We are grateful to Linda Bennett for her work as author, to those who have commented on the text, to Mandy Knight at the PA for her management of the project, and to Libre Digital, who set up the e-book without charge. We commend their services to you.

Graham Taylor
The Publishers Association
August 2010

The Author

Linda Bennett was formerly a director of two library supply companies and Waterstone's. She founded Gold Leaf in 2001, to provide business development advice and market research to the publishing, academic, library and bookselling/book support communities. She undertakes small and large scale research projects, for publishers on a confidential basis; and for government and industry organisations, often for publication.

Although she works in many areas of publishing she specialises particularly in work on e-books, e-learning and e-publishing. *E-Book Aggregators and Platforms* was published in 2006 by ALPSP; *E-Books: the Options* was commissioned and published by The Publishers Association shortly afterwards. She contributed to the work carried out by The Publishers Association for the *Textbook Action Group Survey* (2005) and the 2007 *Open Books, Open Minds initiative*. Other publications include *Promoting the Uptake of E-books in Higher Further Education* (2003 - 2004), which was commissioned by JISC; *Do Textbooks Deliver Value for Money?* (2002), also for The Publishers Association, and *The Independent Booksellers Guide to Multi-Channel Bookselling* (2010), *Booksellers' Remuneration Report* (2004) and *The Net Pricing Report* (2002) for the Booksellers Association.

Linda arranges seminars and conferences for publishers, booksellers and others associated with the industry including organising the speakers for the BA's annual APSBG Conference in March. She has spoken at and arranged a number of e-books seminars, including *Future Present: Changing Your Environment with E-Books*, which she chaired for ALPSP in November 2007, *From Psychosis to Metamorphosis: a History of E-Books*, at The Publishers Association's International Conference in 2008, and *My Plans for World Domination were Sadly Mistaken*, a presentation following a trip to Russia to teach Russian librarians about e-books, at an ALPSP seminar on Eastern Europe in October 2008. She provides advice to those new to the industry, e.g., digital wholesalers and platform providers. She runs five user/advisory groups for publishing and book-trade-related organisations and edits their newsletters. She is a research fellow of Bristol Business School, Manchester Metropolitan University Business School and Huddersfield University Business School (where she was MBA Course Director for three years), and acts as field reporter for The Publishers Association on issues related to e-learning and e-publishing.

Introduction

Background

Since *E-books: the Options* was published by The Publishers Association in 2006, the e-book world has become much more crowded and complex. Formats, platforms, pricing models and new opportunities to take content to market have proliferated. The choices that now confront publishers are bewildering, and opportunity costs can be high. At the same time, some of the fears that publishers expressed initially – about 'cannibalisation' of print sales, for example – are still either unfounded or unproven. Costs of conversion and 'solutions' have reduced significantly. For academic publishers especially, exciting new markets have opened up throughout the world. New ways of accessing content through mobile phones and more sophisticated proprietary e-book readers have attracted new types of customer. New pricing models have enabled publishers to maximise sales of their content. E-books and other forms of electronic publishing, notably Print on Demand, have accelerated development of a 'joined-up' approach to publishing in which the content is produced, edited and exploited in multiple formats through a continuous series of related applications which simultaneously reduce effort and cost and provide greater flexibility.

Despite all of this, however, e-publishing is still in a state of transition. There are two main reasons for this: firstly, content is still being produced by most publishers for the print book first and foremost, so that some of the opportunities unique to digital publishing are not being fully exploited; secondly, publishers' customers, whether they are based in the same country or a different country from the publisher itself, occupy widely differing points on a continuum of demand which requires basic plain text at one end of the spectrum and a fully interactive, sophisticated multimedia 'experience' at the other. As always, the relative investment costs and the prices that customers are willing or prepared to pay are significant factors.

This report, which is intended for use by both trade and academic publishers as part manual, part reference work, part directory, has been divided into three. The first part is both an update of *E-books: the Options* and a survey of the companies that publishers can work with in order to achieve different types of electronic offer (including some sections on audiobooks, Print on Demand, and publishing e-content for the reading impaired). The second part explores specific market opportunities in the Anglophone countries and selected European countries, with the emphasis on those countries which are most likely to use material written in the English language. The third gives contact information about the main library consortia operating throughout the world and contact details of many of the companies featured in Parts One and Two.

Unsurprisingly, there is much more information available about the Anglophone countries than mainland Europe, because, for a variety of reasons, exploitation of e-content in the former colonies is more advanced. In the case of some European countries, only a small amount of reliable information has been discovered; this has therefore been presented in bullet format. Examining digital opportunities in the rest of the world was deemed to be beyond the scope of this first report, but it is hoped that future editions will address other geographical regions, particularly China, the Indian sub-continent, and the rest of South-East Asia.

Development of e-books and key issues

Before embarking upon the main body of the report, it may be helpful to outline the key issues currently being faced by trade and academic publishers respectively as they develop their e-book strategies.

Trade e-publishing

Although trade publishers have been experimenting with e-books for almost as long as academic publishers – indeed, the first e-books to be made commercially available to consumers in the UK were published by HarperCollins on its Fire and Water[1] website in the year 2000 – it is fair to say that they have waited for the commercial availability of user-friendly hand-held readers before fully engaging with the e-book market.

The launch of the Sony e-reader in 2008 and the Amazon Kindle in 2009, followed by the long-promised iPad this year, have therefore been key catalysts in accelerating the digitisation and sale of e-books by trade

1   This is now defunct. HarperCollins now sells e-books from www.harpercollinsebooks.co.uk

publishers. By 2008 all of the leading trade publishers had established strong e-book publishing programmes and their own transactional e-book platforms, and many independent publishers – for example, Bloomsbury and Faber – had also launched their own platforms.

Trade publishers' serious commitment to the e-book format has marked a step-change in electronic publishing for the following reasons:

- It has caused the **publishers to engage directly with consumers**, whereas previously they have mainly relied on booksellers to do this.

- It has therefore **called into question the traditional publisher/ bookseller relationship,** which elements (if any) of it will survive, and if it does survive, how it will be modified.

- To some extent, it has **redefined the nature and reach of the product supplied by the publisher.** There has been a growing recognition that not only is the publisher's task in part to supply e-books to fulfil a component of the lifestyle of the consumer, but that because the Internet as a whole helped to create this lifestyle, publishers may choose or even be obliged to engage in related online activities. For example, Penguin has set up an online dating service on its website; Scholastic has placed downloadable assets aimed at booksellers and parents on its. blogs, podcasts, sign-ups for author events and e-alerts and links to social networks and online bookshops have proliferated on many publishers' websites. E-book tokens are available from publishers themselves and from their channel partners.

- Related to the nature of the product and the publisher's relationship with the consumer is the momentous **problem of discoverability.** With the exception of a few niche publishers, such as Mills & Boon, and the handful of publishers whose names are household words (Penguin, Encyclopaedia Britannica, Oxford University Press), most consumers are not only not interested, but are unaware of the publisher's brand or imprint(s). It is the author who has the brand name, not the publisher. Yet unlike physical books in a bookshop, e-books cannot be browsed unless the consumer is aware of their existence. This means that publishers have to find new ways of marketing the book: hence the advent of the widget and the increasing importance of social networks as promotional tools.

- Much more than with academic publishing, the rise of the trade e-book has immediately put **pressure on the industry's economics.** This has been caused by the dual squeeze of consumer perception that e-books are less valuable than print books[2] , and by the extraordinary power of the main channel partners: particularly Amazon, which has succeeded in reducing most e-books sold on its site to the uniform price of $9.99. Alternative pricing models – e.g., the Apple 'agency' model and the retail subscription model pioneered by Harlequin Mills & Boon – are now being trialled to attempt to find ways of preserving margin.

- It has also **called to account the whole infrastructure of publishing,** i.e., the pyramid of costs incurred by warehousing, physical stock and the notoriously inefficient physical supply chain, as well as the less tangible services that publishers perform. At the same time, it has left publishers exposed to the need to explain how the price charged for a book is broken down, and particularly how to explain the costs and concomitant added value of the editorial, design, marketing and distribution activities which together constitute – and have in fact always constituted – the publisher's core role.

- On the positive side, **trade publishers have been much quicker than academic publishers to unlock the potential of the e-book format,** and to use the technology itself to add value. Children's e-books have been published which incorporate interactive games and puzzles; authors have been encouraged to publish work-in-progress and engage in online 'chat' with their readers; they have been persuaded to give away short stories or previous novels free in order to promote their latest works.

---

2   Academic publishers have fought this battle with some success.

- There is also a negative side to the last point. Stepping up **author engagement with readers** has left a question mark hanging over the role of the author, especially with regard to the fundamental issues of whether expecting authors to engage in continual online dialogue either affects their ability to create or actually devalues their work; and exactly how they will be paid in the future as more and more of their work is delivered 'free'.

- A further negative impact concerns the **increase of piracy**[3], which has proliferated in some trade publishing segments as more digital product has been introduced. This raises the issue of DRM, whether consumers will be prepared to tolerate it, and if not, what safeguards can be put in its place. Consumers are particularly resentful of DRM mechanisms which prevent them from storing a title on two different types of device unless they make two separate purchases of the book.

- Linked to DRM is also the question of **territoriality** – another big plank of traditional trade publishing – and whether it can – and indeed, should - be protected.

There have been eloquent prophets of doom who have predicted that the established trade – and even, perhaps, some of the academic - publishing companies will not survive. It is important to keep an undistorted perspective about this, especially as the larger companies are now all engaging strenuously – and often very imaginatively – with the electronic medium. However, the advent of e-books has introduced some powerful big beasts to the publishing market, the largest of whom – Google, Amazon and Apple - are not competing with publishers on their own terms, since the supply of books constitutes only one facet of their wider agendas.

---

3   Publishers have to exert constant vigilance to protect digital copyright – see for example
    www.baka-tsuki.org/project/index.php?title=Main_Page

Academic and STM e-publishing

Although they had flirted with CD-ROMs and other forms of electronic publishing in the 1980s, academic and STM publishers first started to experiment seriously with e-books after the foundation (in 1997) of NetLibrary, the first of the big general e-book aggregators to make e-books commercially available for sale to libraries. At the same time, some academic and STM publishers realised that putting some of their titles on the themed electroni platforms of secondary publishers, such as those offered by ProQuest, Chadwyck-Healey, Ovid and Gale Reference Online, could yield attractive rewards. Publishers with extensive backlists, like OUP, created their own themed online collections.

Early engagement with the discrete commercial e-book market was cautious [4]. Publishers were at first keen to adopt the 'one book, one user' model which formed the basis of NetLibrary's offer, and which replicated the physical library lending model exactly. They also wanted to charge as much or more for the e-book than the print book: NetLibrary's standard mark-up was +33 per cent of the cover price. Such caution was understandable, as the commercial flaws that had been inadvertently introduced into the electronic journals market some years previously were now becoming apparent. Foremost among these was a pricing model which allowed a library or individual to obtain the electronic version of a journal in addition to the print version for a small surcharge (typically 10 - 20 per cent). As it became clear that journals users would switch relatively rapidly to an electronic-only format, publishers realised that they had not only made the mistake of deeply discounting their principal future revenue streams but also linked their prices to a print model which would eventually become irrelevant. (Journals publishing is still bedevilled by pricing issues.) This made publishers sensitive to making hard-to-rectify mistakes when pricing e-books.

NetLibrary was closely followed into the market by other general aggregators – OverDrive, Ebrary and EBooks Corporation – and some

---

4   Arguably, it was precipitated by initiatives taken by some libraries to download free materials from online collections such as Project Gutenberg.

specialist ones – Safari, Knovel and Books24x7[5]. Some time afterwards, the main academic library suppliers developed their own e-book platforms. Coutts came first with MyiLibrary[6], followed by Blackwell's ECHO and Dawson's DawsonEra. Different pricing models began to evolve in response to demand from librarians.

By the middle of this decade, almost all of the books made available on these various platforms were still either reference works or monographs, and the majority of sales were to libraries [7]. Most of the electronic books supplied were in PDF format, although the ePub format was being developed, and nearly all e-books were more or less reproductions of the print version. A few born-digital books were published, and there were occasional attempts to exploit the technological possibilities of electronic publishing more enterprisingly: for example, Knovel embedded drop-down boxes in some of the titles in its specialised Mathematics and Engineering collections, through which the user could perform and check mathematical calculations. By now publishers were beginning to be confronted with some big questions, as the academic book market moved, more slowly than the academic journals market, it is true, but still inexorably, towards 'digital-preferred' (a term which had begun to appear in university strategy and university library policy documents). The question of greatest strategic significance for publishers was whether to accede to academic demand for digital textbooks, and if so how to price them, especially if they were to be supplied to libraries as well as to individual students (thus eroding the sales potential of the already declining student textbook market). International academic publishers with UK divisions have since experimented with e-textbook platforms in the USA with varying degrees of success, and some e-textbook initiatives are being developed in the UK.

At the time of writing, the future of the textbook has itself turned into a crucial topic. As well as being concerned about pricing and the protection of revenue streams that may be jeopardised by the digitisation

5   All of these companies have survived, and most have continued to thrive, though NetLibrary
    has changed hands several times. One or two other aggregators – for example, Ellibs, a
    Finnish company – have not proved to be as robust.
6   Both Coutts and MyiLibrary are now owned by the Ingram group.
7   EBooks Corporation was the only academic e-book aggregator to develop a consumer division
    – ebooks.com – right from the start.

of textbooks, publishers are acutely aware of the dangers of e-textbook piracy. At the same time, they are trying to accommodate the changing demands of academia. The era of the big 'blockbuster' textbook, which has never been as popular with academics in the UK as it is in the US, would appear to be on the wain. The biggest textbook publishers are now experimenting with e-learning platforms in an attempt to address both the piracy and the declining textbook issues. They and other publishers are also developing specific materials for Virtual Learning Environments (VLEs) and Managed Learning Environments (MLEs).

All of these initiatives have had profound effects on publishers' back-end systems, and the tools for writing and editing books. Many publishers now operate XML-first workflows which can deliver output in all formats. A few have developed their back-end systems and electronic platforms in-house from scratch, but most work with one or more (usually several, often many) digital partners. Therefore, the components of the supply chain itself have changed.

Finally, social networks have affected academic publishing as much as trade publishing, but in different ways. Academic authors are provided with online fora by academic publishers so that they can discuss topics relating to their research, and also write collaboratively if they wish. Students use public social networks to exchange ideas about books, and they maintain contact with both academics and their course peers by using their universities' own social networks. Widgets are effective in sharing information about books through social networks, and thus generating sales for publishers.

The key issues for academic-e-publishing are:

- How far and how fast academic publishers should move from print to electronic while at the same time attempting to preserve steady revenue streams.

- Pricing models and business models are inextricably linked with the point above. Publishers have to develop innovative ways of charging the library market that librarians will find both affordable and attractive as their budgets are squeezed. Retail prices for students also have to be attractive, and the material has to be relevant to their needs – which may mean offering content on a 'slice-and-dice' or per-chapter basis.

- A further associated issue (already mentioned) is the **decline of the print textbook** and whether or not to attempt to halt this by making textbooks available electronically (taking into account the possible risks.

- **Whether or not to put a DRM wrap-around on digital books** is perhaps an even thornier issue for academic publishers than it is for trade publishers. Academic publishers are aware that students are likely to engage in file-sharing if this is possible. On the other hand, DRM annoys both students and librarians because it makes the electronic reading experience relatively 'clunky'. They also dislike the 'lock-outs' created by some DRM systems when pages are clicked through too rapidly (because they are set to register that copyright abuse is then taking place). As with trade consumers, academic consumers resent the fact that DRM makes downloading the same purchase on two different kinds of hardware impossible. It is a brave textbook publisher who decides not to protect e-textbooks with DRM; but some academic publishers are now experimenting with **'social copyright protection'** (i.e., a requirement to observe terms and conditions of use, often accompanied by digital watermarking) for monographs. All academic publishers are aware that even the most robust DRM systems are not infallible, and that the print format is almost as vulnerable to piracy.

- **Customer perception of the worth of electronic 'added value'** has been driven downwards by both the proliferation of 'free' material on the web and, more recently, the deep discounting of e-books that has taken place in the trade consumer market. Even more than for trade publishers, there is scope for academic publishers to exploit technological innovation to add value in ways that can not be replicated either in print or by online materials delivered free of charge. The difficulty lies in assessing what the market is prepared to pay. Students, in particular, may feel that 'penny plain' and free is 'good enough'. Authenticity is perhaps the most important value-add created by publishers, but students often do not recognise this. At the opposite end of the academic publishing spectrum from textbooks, the publication of specialist monographs is becoming increasingly difficult to make financially viable. Creating them 'born digital' can help, but only if the minority market at which they are aimed is still prepared to pay a premium over other electronic products.

- As well as making the decision of whether or not to develop their own e-book platforms instead of or as well as placing books with aggregators, publishers are recognising that they also have to decide **whether it should be a multi-product platform** – i.e., capable of hosting both e-books and journals and any other types of electronic content that they might supply (such as 'middleware' or database products). From the customer's point of view, particularly if the customer is a librarian, a multi-product platform is almost always to be preferred, provided that it is easy to navigate. From the publisher's point of view, an all-inclusive approach may make business models complicated or sales less profitable than if kept separate for different formats (and sometimes difficult to implement because of internal structures and systems procedures).

- As for trade publishers, digital publishing is changing the **publisher's relationship with the author.** The academic publisher/author relationship has always been complex, because of the author's dual role as producer and consumer of the publisher's output. Increasingly, the academic author's employer is becoming a passive but observant third in this relationship. Some universities now monitor more strictly how academics spend their time, and demands are being made for materials developed during academics' contractual hours to be 'owned' by the university or placed within its institutional repository. Open Access models for monographs are already being explored.

- **Discoverability** presents a challenge to academic as well as to trade publishers. It is less of a problem in the library market, since publishers, library suppliers and e-book aggregators are all quite successful in forging strong relationships with librarians, and can then set up e-mail alerts and RSS feeds to advise them of new products and publications (although librarians frequently complain of information overload and the information may not always reach the right person). But reaching students in order to provide information about e-books and so generate sales is fraught with difficulties. It is heavily dependent on the willingness of lecturers and librarians to include URL links on VLEs and in reading lists. Universities will generally not give publishers and other e-book sellers direct contact details for students.

Part One | Choices

1.1   E-book formats

The proliferation of e-book formats has been described as the 'Tower of eBabel'. In some ways it is unhelpful that there are so many formats to choose from; on the other hand, each format has unique characteristics or cost advantages that make it fit for certain purposes. The following is a brief description of the main formats supported by publishers in the Anglophone countries and Europe. The list is by no means exhaustive, but it does cover at least 90 per cent of what is in common use in the e-book sector.

1.1.1   Adobe Portable Document (PDF)

Adobe PDF is still the most common format for e-books, though it is gradually being superseded by XML applications, particularly ePub, which is becoming the industry standard. The PDF format specification is available free of charge from Adobe.

The key feature of the PDF format as it was originally developed is that it has been designed to reproduce images of the printed page. This means that the text cannot be reflowed to fit the screen width of small devices. Therefore, files originally designed for printing on standard paper sizes are not easily viewed on mobile phones and some proprietary hand-held readers. Adobe has, in fact, addressed the problem by adding a re-flow facility to its Acrobat Reader software, but this cannot be introduced retrospectively: the document has to be marked for re-flowing when it is first created. The Windows Mobile[8] version of Adobe Acrobat will automatically attempt to tag a PDF for re-flow during the synchronisation process. However, it will not work on most locked PDF documents. If Windows Vista is being used with a Windows Mobile device and Adobe Acrobat, the tagging process must occur before the device is synchronised.

Multiple Adobe products support creating PDF files, such as Adobe Acrobat and Adobe Capture, as do third-party products such as

---

8   Also known as Pocket PC

PDFCreator and OpenOffice.org. Adobe Reader[9] is the application developed by Adobe to view PDF files. There are also third-party versions, such as XPDF. Mac OS X has built-in PDF support, both for creation as part of the printing system and for display using the built-in Preview application. Later versions of Adobe have enabled improved functionality, such as annotation, hypertext links, and even interactive buttons for triggering sound and video (though these features are often not supported by older or third-party viewers, and may not be transferable to print).

As well as on PCs, PDF files may be viewed on the following e-book readers: Sony Reader, Bookeen Cybook, Foxit eSlick and Amazon Kindle DX.

1.1.2   ePub[10]

ePub is the e-book standard that has been developed by the International Digital Publishing Forum (IDPF). It is a more sophisticated version of the Open eBook standard, and became the official standard of the IDPF in September 2007. It is a free and open standard for re-flowable content. The great advantage of this, as e-book readers and other 'hardware' devices proliferate, is that the text can be adapted to fit the display area of the screen in question. It is built on xhtml or DTBook (an XML standard developed by the Daisy Consortium[11]).

ePub works with the following software: Adobe Digital Editions; Mobipocket Reader/Creator; Openberg Lector; Stanza Desktop/iTel: (Microsoft, OSX); Aldiko Android smartphones; FBReader Free[12]; Worldplayer Free Reader[13]; Atlantis Word Processor ePub creator for Windows.

As well as on PCs, ePub files may be viewed on the following e-book readers: Cybook Gen 3; Cybook Opus; Apple iPhone[14]; Apple iPad; Hanlin eReader; Sony Reader; all phones or devices using Android; BeBook; jetBook.

---

9   Formerly called Adobe Acrobat Reader
10   Stands for 'Electronic Publication'. Also known as IDPF / EPub and OEBPS format.
11   www.daisy.org
12   Open Source multi-format reader for Windows, Linux, etc..
13   For Android (Google) phones
14   Using Lexcycle Stanza

1.1.3　Hypertext Markup Language (.html)

.html is the mark-up language used for most web pages. E-books using .html can be read using a web browser. The format specifications of .html are available free of charge from the World Wide Web Consortium (W3C)[15]. .html adds tagged metadata elements to plain text, using character sets such as ASCII[16] or UTF-8[17]. .html is not a particularly efficient information storage format, as it requires a great deal of space. It does not describe pages (as per the print page) and cannot store multiple elements (e.g., text plus images) in a single file. E-books created in the .html format are often stored on a file per chapter basis.

1.1.4　Kindle (.azw)

Amazon created the AZW format for the Kindle. It is based on the Mobipocket standard, with a different serial scheme[18], and its own DRM formatting. E-books bought for the Kindle are delivered wirelessly via a system which Amazon calls Whispernet[19].

1.1.5　Mobipocket

The Mobipocket e-book format is based on the Open eBook standard using xhtml and can include JavaScript and frames. It also supports native SQL queries to be used with embedded databases. There is a corresponding e-book reader - the Mobipocket Reader - which has a home page library. Readers can add blank pages to any part of a book for annotation/freehand drawing. Highlights, bookmarks, corrections, notes and drawings can be applied, organised and recalled from a single location. Mobipocket Reader has electronic bookmarks and a built-in dictionary.

As well as being readable on PCs, the reader has a full screen mode for reading and support for many PDAs, Communicators and Smartphones. Mobipocket supports most Windows, Symbian, Blackberry and Palm

---

15　www.w3.org
16　www.asciitable.com
17　www.cl.cam.ac.uk/~mgk25/unicode.html
18　It uses an asterisk instead of the dollar sign
19　It is in fact EvDO – see - www.evdoinfo.com/content/view

operating systems. The Amazon Kindle's AZW format is essentially the Mobipocket format.

1.1.6 Microsoft Lit (.lit)

The Microsoft Reader uses proprietary ClearType display technology. DRM protected .lit files are only readable via the (also proprietary) Microsoft Reader programme. Unprotected .lit files can be read through a small range of third party readers, such as Lexcycle Stanza. The user can add annotations and notes to any page, create large print e-books, and create free-form drawings on the reader pages. There is a built-in dictionary.

1.1.7 Palm eReader (.pdb)

eReader is a freeware program for viewing Palm Digital Media electronic books. Versions are available for iPhone, Palm OS, Symbian, Blackberry, Windows Mobile Pocket PC/Smartphone, desktop Windows and Macintosh. The Stanza application for the iPhone and iPod Touch can read both encrypted and unencrypted eReader files. The eReader reproduces the look and feel of the print page.

The program supports features such as bookmarks and footnotes. Footnotes can later be exported as a Memo document. There is support for an integrated reference dictionary (many options are available), for which any word in the text can be highlighted and looked up in the dictionary.

In July 2009 Barnes and Noble announced that the eReader format would be the method they would use to deliver e-books. Updated versions of the Palm Digital programs for Apple iPhone/iTouch/iPad, Blackberry, Mac OS X and Windows platforms are now available on the Barnes and Noble website [20].

---

20   www.barnesandnoble.com/ebooks/download-reader.asp?cds2Pid=29168&linkid=1445802

1.2   XML and the future

It will have been noted that many, but not all, of the formats described above are XML based. XML[21] is a flexible method for marking up structured documents. The mark-up's prime purpose is to indicate the purpose of the content. It is therefore essential if the publisher wishes to make its e-books fully searchable. It has variously been described as the 'building blocks' and the 'DNA' of publishing, and while neither of these analogies is exactly precise, each helps to portray the role of XML in making content as flexible and exploitable (in academic parlance 're-purposable') as possible.

As publishers become more confident of the power of content over format, and as e-books become more accepted as simply another format that should be offered as part of the publisher's mainstream repertoire, producing all content in XML from inception will become the publisher's goal. Using XML from the start makes the publishing process cheaper and more flexible, resulting in more opportunities to take content to market, and increases the publisher's range of options when selecting platform partners and other third parties with whom it wishes to operate[22].

1.3   E-readers

It has long been recognised that the most significant development needed in order to promote e-books successfully to the consumer market would be the creation of a user-friendly, affordable device on which to read them. In the past eighteen months, there has been a proliferation of such devices, culminating in the launch of Apple's iPad in the USA and UK.

E-readers come in three main categories: multi-purpose devices such as PCs, Netbooks and SmartPhones; several-purpose devices such as tablets and Mobile Internet Devices (MIDs); and dedicated e-readers as shown in Figure 1.1.

---

21 The acronym stands for Extensible Markup Language
22 More about XML may be found at www.w3schools.com/XML/xml_whatis.asp

Figure 1.1 The spectrum of ereader devices

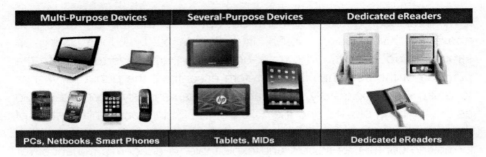

Source: Libre Digital Presentation at London Book Fair 2010

Keeping up with which devices are available in which countries and their respective technical attributes and prices is a challenge. Various sources of help are available online, the best of which is probably Wikipedia's E-Book Reader Matrix for e-book reader devices that use e-paper[23] and its LCD E-Book Reader Matrix[24]. Wikipedia has also developed a matrix for web tablets[25], an information page about PDA devices[26] which includes a summary of the features of the iPad[27], and a shorter, incomplete page on SmartPhones[28]. Blogs on e-readers are numerous. The most-visited ones are listed at E-Reader Blog Posts[29].

As most e-readers were first launched in North America, and many more are available for purchase there than elsewhere in the world, most of the reliable statistics relating to them also come from the US. The Book Industry Study Group has carried out a consumer survey which captures the change in reading habits of people who have acquired hand-held readers (see Figure 1.2).

Despite the huge improvements that have been made recently to enhance the e-reading experience, however, e-readers are still in the early stages of development, and users still experience problems. As part of the same

23 See http://wiki.mobileread.com/wiki/E-book_Reader_Matrix#Matrix_.28epaper_devices.29
24 See http://wiki.mobileread.com/wiki/LCD_E-Book_Reader_Matrix.
25 See http://wiki.mobileread.com/wiki/Web_Tablet
26 See http://wiki.mobileread.com/wiki/PDA_devices
27 See http://wiki.mobileread.com/wiki/IPad
28 See http://wiki.mobileread.com/wiki/Smartphones
29 See www.blogtopsites.com/post/e+reader

research exercise, the Book Industry Study Group also sought to capture these (see Figure 1.3)

Figure 1.2 Changes in readers' habits once having acquired an e-reader

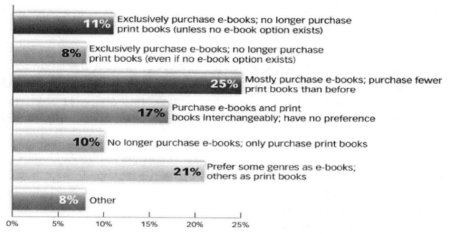

11%	Exclusively purchase e-books; no longer purchase print books (unless no e-book option exists)
8%	Exclusively purchase e-books; no longer purchase print books (even if no e-book option exists)
25%	Mostly purchase e-books; purchase fewer print books than before
17%	Purchase e-books and print books interchangeably; have no preference
10%	No longer purchase e-books; only purchase print books
21%	Prefer some genres as e-books; others as print books
8%	Other

Source: Book Industry Study Group's Consumer *Attitudes Toward E-Book Reading survey*"[30]

Figure 1.3 Most significant problems cited by digital content consumers

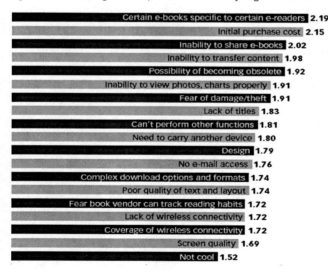

Certain e-books specific to certain e-readers	2.19
Initial purchase cost	2.15
Inability to share e-books	2.02
Inability to transfer content	1.98
Possibility of becoming obsolete	1.92
Inability to view photos, charts properly	1.91
Fear of damage/theft	1.91
Lack of titles	1.83
Can't perform other functions	1.81
Need to carry another device	1.80
Design	1.79
No e-mail access	1.76
Complex download options and formats	1.74
Poor quality of text and layout	1.74
Fear book vendor can track reading habits	1.72
Lack of wireless connectivity	1.72
Coverage of wireless connectivity	1.72
Screen quality	1.69
Not cool	1.52

Source: Book Industry Study Group's *Consumer Attitudes Toward E-Book Reading survey*"[31]

30   See www.bisg.org/publications/product.php?p=19&c=437
31   www.bisg.org/publications/product.php?p=19&c=437

The most controversial issue captured here is also the one with the most far-reaching consequences for the publishing industry. It concerns certain *e-books specific to certain e-readers*; *inability to share e-books*; and *inability to share content*. With one important variation, these three descriptors all relate to the same issue: Digital Rights Management (whether it is introduced through the e-reader operating via a proprietary format, or whether a DRM wrapper has been placed around the e-book). The general reluctance of the consumer market to accept the limitations imposed by DRM – which has been unpopular but more or less accepted by the institutional market for the last ten years – has obliged publishers to think about how necessary it really is, and how they can combat piracy and illegal file-sharing without it.

The important variation which differentiates the three descriptors above informs the decision-making process. Publishers are likely to be sympathetic to the frustrations associated with certain e-books being specific to certain e-readers if the person who has purchased the title owns two or more devices - a PC and an iPad, for example – and wants to place the same content on both without making a second purchase of the title. The purchase of a television licence offers an analogy. If two or more televisions exist in the same household, they still only require one licence. *Inability to transfer content* may also relate to this; but it may also relate to *inability to share e-books* – which is certainly something that publishers wish to discourage. 'Sharing' implies sharing with another person – i.e., file-sharing – which is illegal and obviously erodes sales.

1.4   Cataloguing e-books

Making e-books visible is not such an acute problem as it was in 2006, when *E-Books: the Options* was published; however, it is still the case that there is no one standard source of information for e-books. The following now have extensive e-book catalogues:

- **Nielsen BookData.** For publishers seeking an international market for their e-books, NBD operates in more than 70 countries, and is particularly strong in Australia, New Zealand and Asia Pacific, as well as the UK[32].

---

32 See www.nielsenbookdataonline.com/bdol

- **Bowker.** Bowker now also lists e-books extensively. It is particularly strong in the USA, the UK, Australia and New Zealand[33].

- **Library suppliers.** Each of the main UK and US library suppliers has a sophisticated search and order service which allows librarians to see titles in all formats, including electronic, on the same 'page'. Prominent in the UK, US, the Netherlands and Canada, the Coutts Library and Information Services system is called OASIS. Dawson Books (with a substantial customer base in the UK and mainland Europe, especially Scandinavia) has Enterbooks. Each also offers an aggregated e-book platform. The Coutts platform is MyiLibrary, the aggregated platform owned by its parent, Ingram; the Dawson platform is Dawson Era. Both co-operate with publishers to offer special deals and promotions for e-book collections, new titles, etc. In the US, Baker & Taylor has recently started to host digital content. It also has some presence in the UK and is strong in Mexico and Australia; and is developing links with mainland Europe.

- **Amazon and other online booksellers.** Amazon.com lists a huge selection of e-books[34] available for retail purchase for uploading on the Kindle. Amazon.co.uk sells various types of handheld reader and provides links to e-book retailers. The Book Depository[35] lists more than 340,000 e-books on its website.

- **OCLC's World Cat**[36] has an extensive and regularly updated e-books catalogue.

- **Traditional booksellers.** In the UK, Waterstone's website now offers an extensive selection of e-books for download on the Sony e-book reader[37]. John Smith's website offers a large range of academic e-book downloads, including an impressive e-book

33   See www.bowker.com/index.php/component/content/article/8/93
34   www.amazon.com/Kindle;
35   www.bookdepository.co.uk/category/3390/eBooks
36   www.worldcat.org
37   www.waterstones.com/waterstonesweb/navigate.do?ctx=10030

collection[38]. Specialist bookshops such as Hammicks Legal Information Services are now offering e-books, some of them in 'bundled' collections by arrangement with the publisher[39]. Independent booksellers are also experimenting with e-book sales, some of them achieving success with the very affordable Gardner's solution for booksellers. Most of the American chain booksellers offer e-book downloads from their websites. Some European booksellers are also experimenting with downloads, although mainland Europe has been hampered in the retail sector by there being few handheld readers available for sale (a situation which will change in the near future).

- **Wholesalers.** Gardners Books[40] in the UK and Centraal Boekhuis[41] in the Netherlands are two examples of wholesalers who offer a 'white label' platform for booksellers to sell e-books to the retail market.

- **Publishers' own websites.** As mentioned in the Introduction, publishers are not only selling collections of e-books from their own websites, but also setting up parallel services via the sites and using them to get closer to customers. The main obstacle, particularly for trade publishers, lies in driving people to the sites in the first place, except for the handful of publishers whose brand-names are household words.

- **The Digital Book Index**[42] provides links to more than 145,000 e-book titles from commercial and non-commercial publishers, universities and various private sites. It is particularly strong on content designed for the American market.

- **Google.** Publishers will have their own views about whether or not a working relationship with Google is beneficial. For publishers who believe that it is, Google hosts an extensive

---

38   www.jscampus.co.uk/shop/ebooks.asp?
39   www.hammickslegal.co.uk/shop
40   www.gardners.com/gardners/Default.aspx
41   www.centraal.boekhuis.nl
42   www.digitalbookindex.org/about.htm

collection of e-books for purchase for use on the Android and iPhone[43], as well as providing links to commercial e-tailers.

1.5   Tagging and metadata

Just as crucial as the ability to locate e-books in the first place is the development of the means to search their content. This is much more important than for print books, because e-books are essentially 'invisible' – they cannot be browsed at random except via the utilisation of (necessarily sophisticated) technology. The need becomes even more imperative when large collections of e-books are involved. For example, Oxford Scholarship Online (OSO) has the following features incorporated into it to aid searching: metadata, abstracts, keywords and MARC records; plus additional functionality to assist searching, cross-referencing and linking from references using Open URLs and DOIs. The collection can also be searched externally via Google, OPAC systems in academic libraries, etc.

Metadata is information that is held about a particular piece of data or content. There are different metadata formats, but they all have in common that they are structured around a set of keywords and data category descriptions. Consistent use of metadata is an invaluable aid to locating material within e-books and making users and potential users aware of basic information about their content.

There have been increasingly sophisticated attempts to create metadata standards. A simple but widespread standard is that established by the Dublin Core Metadata Initiative (DCMI) - www.dublincore.org.

The international standard for book metadata in the commercial publishing world (based on a much more sophisticated model than Dublin Core) is ONIX – www.editeur.org/onix.html. This is rapidly increasing in use in the USA and UK, and is also being adopted in other European and English-speaking countries. ONIX is also being piloted as a standard by RROs and other organisations key to the book industry. Ideally, publishers of e-books should be capable of producing metadata to the ONIX standard, which enables them to include specific e-product codes that distinguish between all known formats for both hand-held and PC-

43 http://books.google.com/m

based e-books. ONIX has been mapped to MARC 21 by the Library of Congress and to UNIMARC by the British Library. ONIX can also be mapped into DCMI, but since this is much more basic, some valuable information would almost certainly be lost in the process.

1.6 Marc 21 records

Publishers often find MARC records both mysterious and irritating. This format has been used by librarians for cataloguing purposes for decades, and the standard has been updated periodically – the latest version is called "MARC 21". For more information about MARC records visit: www.loc.gov/marc/specifications/spechome.html

Also, CILIP, the librarians' association in the UK, frequently runs seminars and lectures on the subject – see www.cilip.org.uk.

Although the detail may be baffling, there is no need for publishers to be totally mystified by MARC. There are some similarities between ONIX and MARC, but it is important to understand what the differences are. ONIX was created to provide information to support trading in books, and includes rich descriptive information about the product as well as supplying details to facilitate trading, such as price and availability. MARC is entirely concerned with cataloguing library resources; it is structured in a very different way from ONIX, and is highly prescriptive in terms of cataloguing rules and authority (where ONIX is very permissive). To produce a valid MARC record, it is essential to observe Anglo-American Cataloguing Rules (AACR2) – for more information about these, see www.aacr2.org. Publishers would find this degree of specificity extremely hard to attain. At the same time, having grown out of a very flat "catalogue card" format, MARC has had to be developed in ways that can seem random and unstructured to the uninitiated.

ONIX can be partially mapped to MARC (and MARC to ONIX); but publishers are unlikely to wish to adopt all elements of AACR2 (some of which look a little odd to non-librarian eyes) to create a valid record. However, some library customers are expecting publishers to provide MARC records, particularly with e-books, so publishers will need to be able to source valid MARC. OCLC has announced a service for converting

ONIX records to MARC and vice versa, and publishers may find this (and similar mechanisms for creating MARC) useful in order to meet the market demand.

Libraries are aware of the need to upgrade their cataloguing practice, and have been developing an approach based on Functional Requirements for Bibliographic Records (FRBR), usually pronounced "fur-bur"). The replacement for AACR2 is called RDA ("Resource Description and Access") and remains under development. This will take an approach to cataloguing that is structurally very much closer to ONIX, almost certainly making mappings more successful, although there will always be fundamental differences in purpose for use (between selling books and cataloguing them). It will also be a long time before FRBR-isation of library catalogues becomes common - MARC is extremely well embedded.

1.7   E-books and ISBNS

An inconsistency of practice (especially in the USA) has emerged around the "correct" way in which to allocate ISBNs to e-books. In part this has been caused by the logical, if counter-intuitive, requirement that e-versions of the same book in different formats should have different ISBNs, just as paperback and hardback print books do but with less certainty about what constitutes a "product" in digital form; in part by a practice that has grown up in some publishing houses of referring to an eISBN, which is not technically incorrect, can be misleading and is actively deprecated by the International ISBN agency; or using the term 'eISBN' as a kind of master-label for all of the different e-book versions of the same title, which is certainly incorrect.

At the time of writing, research is in hand to try to resolve these issues, but in the meantime, Peter Mathews of Nielsen BookData explains the view of his company:

> *"Certainly one thing the term eISBN does not mean is that it is a different type of ISBN that can only be used for e-books or similar: ISBNs are ISBNs and can apply to (and should be applied to) any, separately tradable 'book' product, whether that is a physical or digital product. The iSBN works as a unique standard identifier*

that is able to be assigned by (and therefore attributed to) the publisher of the product and can therefore represent that product (with suitable metadata) within the supply chain.

One other thing that the term eISBN should not be used for (but unfortunately is sometimes) is as a generic identifier for an e-book 'master' record, i.e., the primary content file that is reformatted into a range of file formats to create actual, saleable products. The ISBN that might be assigned to this 'master' record so that it can be added to a publisher's system is sometimes referred to as the eISBN. Different publishers then take different views on whether they then need also to number the separate products that are derived from this master record with a separate ISBN for each product. Our unequivocal advice to publishers is that each separately tradable product should be identified separately with a separate ISBN, and that each of these should have a separate product record in our database. In fact these are the only digital product records we will allow on to the Nielsen Bookdata database (which is, after all, a product database) - we will not accept the 'master' record since it is not a tradable product."

Further confusion has been caused more recently, as retail e-book sales have grown, by the suggestion from some quarters that a separate ISBN is needed for e-books supplied to each **vendor** or third party aggregator. This is considered by Nielsen Bookdata to be unnecessary.

For publishers seeking guidance, Nielsen Bookdata has posted a e-book policy document[44] on its website that gives clear advice.

---

44 www.nielsenbookdata.co.uk/uploads/NielsenBook_EBookPolicyDocument_Aug08.pdf

1.8 Digital Object Identifiers (DOIs)

At the simplest level, the DOI is a number that identifies content of all types, including entire publications or parts of publications (such as individual chapters, images, articles, directory entries and so on). The DOI shares many of the characteristics of the ISBN and also the Internet URL. Like the ISBN, the DOI acts as a unique, unambiguous identifier. As with an ISBN, the prefix is unique to the owner of the publication and the suffix to the individual content. It may be described as a signpost or grid reference for the Internet, one that tells you where to find some content and takes you to it as well.

The supply-chain model for electronic publications is still in its infancy compared to that for print-publications, and so far there is no clear vision of where the majority of consumers will go to discover and obtain digital publications. However, one certainty is that no publication is likely to have any sales unless it can be reliably identified and located on the Internet. Unfortunately neither of the 'traditional' solutions is adequate on its own. An ISBN could identify the desired publication, but consumers will typically wish to download it and need to know where they can obtain a copy. At present, there is no consumer-facing equivalent of the Teleordering system for locating the current outlet and 'ordering' (i.e. downloading) a copy of the publication, but such a system could be built around DOIs. A URL can be used to promote the Internet location from where a publication can be downloaded, but URLs so often become out of date when websites are redeveloped and systems-providers (and their computers) are changed. The DOI system has therefore been developed to enable publishers to have control of where the references from third-party sites lead to. Unfortunately, so far publishers have been slow to incorporate DOIs into their e-books.

Nielsen BookData formally ceased to be a DOI registration agency in May 2009, having offered the service for more than three years. The simple reason for this was that it encountered no demand for DOIs within the book industry; it says that this was because there were (and still are) no applications which require what the DOI has to offer. Nielsen will continue to monitor the situation, so that if a genuine book-trade business application requiring the use of DOIs becomes apparent, it might consider offering registration services again.

However, DOIs may still be obtained from CrossRef (www.crossref.org) and from mEDRA (www.medra.org), the European multi-lingual DOI agency. The International DOI Foundation (www.doi.org) maintains a list of authorised Registration Agencies, who will register content and provide services using DOIs.

1.9   The 'Semantic Web' (Web 3.0)

The 'semantic web', or Web 3.0, is an umbrella term used to describe using artificial intelligence to locate publications on the Internet. At present it the concept is mainly being explored within the context of academic publishing. Its underlying rationale is that although everyone starts with Google, the keyword leading to a publication is often ultimately found in a variety of resources: the library OPAC, or an online archive, or an aggregated collection, or a programme delivered via a media site (e.g., the BBC), or the electronic version of a reading list.   Therefore, students and academics are often directed to access content through URLs when better routes could be found. Students and academics generally do not care how they access material: they just want the resource. The following are the ways available of 'getting the answer': via Google Search; via OPAC; by computing the answers – e.g., through Wolfram Alpha; by navigation – e.g., via a pre-release delivered by the Open Library. All of these options are powered by metadata.

Libraries have been delivering metadata for a long time: it is simply a term for information about stuff that the library holds. Often it is locally managed, and often influenced by local practice or copied from shared resources. Metadata has its limitations in the e-world, because it is built on premises that have worked well for physical resources, but have a limited value for their electronic counterparts. The key issue with regard to metadata is that it is only available from the library – either online or through a physical web of linked data. The involution of the web links data together, rather than documents. Libraries have yet to exploit fully the possibilities that this opens up. For example, if a user conducts a search taking Shakespeare as both a subject and a creator, in most library systems the result will be two library records with no relationship mapped between them. They simply act as identifiers for each concept: a string of words associated with them will have been broken out. The identifiers are URLs.

The 'semantic web' does not work like this. It brings data from one place to another to add value; this is fundamentally different from the data that is displayed by the library, which is 'hand-crafted'. An example is offered by the BBC: the BBC does not draft the words that appear under certain topics on its website, but uses the Wikipedia definition. If the latter is considered to be incorrect in any respect, the BBC will go on to the Wikipedia website and correct it; but it will not break out of the interconnected circle of information.

This is what Open Linked data is about; it links data from different respectable websites. It is already used by some avant garde libraries: e.g., at the Library of Congress, no single set of subject headings is adhered to. The idea is that an understanding of the concept under discussion is common or shared. Publishers should encourage librarians to use this type of resource, as it undoubtedly enhances the discoverability of their publications. The semantic web is likely to become much more important to the industry in the future.

1.10   Markets: customers and their needs and wants

1.10.1 The retail market

The retail e-book market is now growing massively, thanks to the recent development of much more sophisticated hand-held readers and 'smart' mobile phones. The e-book reader market is proliferating so quickly that it is difficult for publishers and booksellers to keep up with all the models available. A list[45] of the most important ones can be found in Section 3.1, though it is not exhaustive; and not all models are available worldwide; some cannot be purchased outside the USA. However, some major players have now emerged, and these are covered in a little more detail in this section.

---

45 I am indebted to Sydney Davies of the Booksellers Association for assembling much of the
     material in this list.

iPad

The iPad is a tablet computer designed and developed by Apple. It is

larger than a smartphone and smaller than a laptop. It is manufactured by Foxconn, which also manufactures Apple's iPod, iPhone and Mac Mini in its plant in Shenzhen, China. It has been designed expressly for the purpose of reading e-books and other publications, watching films, listening to music and playing games, and it also incorporates many of the features of a laptop. Thus it can be used to access the Internet, receive and send e-mails, etc. This addresses one of the most commonly-expressed dissatisfactions with hand-held readers: that because they are single-purpose devices, anyone using them has also to carry around a mobile phone, a laptop, etc. However, there are some important features missing from the first generation iPad, including a camera for video chat, Adobe Flash support, a longer and narrower 'widescreen' aspect ratio for watching widescreen films, the ability to multi-task, a USB port, etc. Apple itself says that multi-tasking will be available to all iPad users via a software update by Autumn 2010, and defends the omission of the other features by pointing out that including these would make significant inroads into the iPad's currently impressive ten-hour battery life.

The iPad runs the same operating system as the iPod Touch and iPhone. One of its most distinctive features is that it is controlled by a multi-touch display screen instead of a stylus. It runs iPad-specific applications as well as those written for the iPhone and iPod Touch. It runs proprietary software, software downloaded from Apple's App Store, and software written by developers who have paid for a developer's licence on registered devices. The iPad runs almost all third-party iPhone applications, displaying them at iPhone size or enlarging them to fill the iPad's screen.

E-books are downloaded from the optional iBooks application that can be downloaded from the App Store. The user can then display books and other content in ePub format downloaded from the Apple iBookstore. Most of the major trade publishers have committed to supplying e-books to the iPad, as well as several well-known magazines and newspapers. The iPad incorporates strict DRM control. This includes enabling Apple to disable remotely or delete apps., media or data on the iPad at will. Apple's App store also imposes censorship of content on publishers. Apple is seeking to persuade publishers to use its 'agency model' pricing structure.

Kindle

Kindle is a software and hardware e-book platform developed by Amazon. To date it has developed three hardware devices which support the platform, the Kindle, Kindle 2 and the Kindle DX. Kindle software applications exist for Windows, iOS, Blackberry, Mac OS X and Android. Kindle uses E Ink and electronic paper. It downloads content over Amazon's Whispernet. Most of the content supplied is therefore in iproprietary format – though the Kindle DX, which has a larger screen than the  earlier models, supports simple PDF files. It has been marketed as more suitable than the others for displaying newspaper and textbook content.

Its terms of use forbid owners of the Kindle from transferring Amazon e-books to another device or user. Users can select e-books by using the Kindle itself or via a computer from the Amazon Kindle Store, which now lists more than half a million titles. Many e-books are sold for $9.99 or less. Paid content for the Kindle can also be purchased from approved third parties, e.g., Fictionwise, Mobipocket[46] and Webscriptions. Titles available free of charge can be obtained via providers operating within the public domain – e.g., Project Gutenberg, the World Public Library.

Sony

Sony has also developed a joint software/hardware product. It has launched several hardware e-book readers, the last of which, the Sony

---

46   Amazon owns Mobipocket.

PRS 600 / 900 Reader, was first sold in August 2009. It uses an electronic paper display developed by E Ink and is viewable in direct sunlight. It has a touchscreen. It can also be used as an MP3 player. Officially, owners of the Sony are not allowed to share e-books they have bought; however, five users can be registered to a single account.

Formats supported by the Sony Reader included DRM-protected secure PDF and ePub, and several types of DRM-free text, including DRM-free PDF and ePub. Since August 2009, Sony has sold only ePub e-books from the Sony Reader Store. It no longer uses the proprietary DRM that it originally developed, and has replaced this with Adobe's CS4 server side copy protection, which is in common use throughout the industry.

The Sony comes bundled with Sony's proprietary software (the Sony eBook Library – it was originally called Sony Connect). It is similar to iTunes in nature and requires Windows XP, Windows Vista or Windows 7, an 800 MHz processor, 128MB of RAM and 20MB of hard disk space. Sony also released an official Mac OS X client for the Reader with the release of the PRS-300 and PRS-600. It is not officially supported on Linux-bases systems or other operating systems.

Blio

Another e-book platform that is likely to be a significant long-term survivor

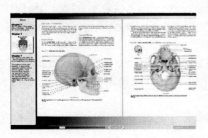

is the Blio. The Blio reader is at present a software product only – there is no accompanying device to complement it, although this may follow eventually. At present the Blio download for PCs and iPhones is available free of charge from the Blio website[47]. What makes it stand out is that it has been developed by KNFB Reading Technology[48], a

---

47 www.blioreader.com
48 www.knfbreader.com

company that specialises in making print more accessible for anyone who has reading difficulties. Blio therefore enables the display of beautiful graphics and operates in colour. Audiobooks can be integrated with their electronic counterparts. Web content can be integrated with e-books. Publishers of children's books and illustrated textbooks have said that the Blio displays their publications especially effectively.

Blio content is acquired via a 'storefront' that is built into the application. Its DRM technology allows the user to download to up to five devices (although it is not possible to deactivate one device in order to add a new one). More than one million e-book titles (both commercially-available and 'free') can be accessed via the Blio.

Blio is based on Microsoft technologies, including XPS (XML Paper Specification) and Windows presentation format. Support for devices other than PCs and iPhones are supplied via Microsoft's Silverlight browser technology.

Emerging e-book readers

Google is working with Verizon, the largest US wireless company, to develop a tablet computer to rival Apple's iPad.

A further significant development will be the advent of colour e-book readers. A Dutch company called Liquavista is already experimenting with a prototype.

1.10.2 The library market

Public libraries

Public libraries in the UK have begun to experiment with e-publications, though coverage is patchy and only a few suppliers are used at present. Oxford University Press has been extremely successful in selling some of its online collections direct to public libraries. Most other publishers approach public libraries through aggregators – OverDrive has a high profile in the UK public library market – or through library suppliers. UK public libraries currently spend about £95m on books and about £7m on newspapers and periodicals annually. The print – electronic split is not recorded, but it is unlikely that electronic publications account for more than 2-3 per cent of these figures. However, this is likely to change – and the public library acquisition of e-books is likely to be accelerated by the government's *Digital Economy Act* (see Section 2.2.3).

Academic libraries

The academic library market is still by far the most lucrative source of income available from e-books to academic publishers. In the Anglophone countries, many academic libraries now have a 'digital-preferred' policy, meaning that the library will buy the e-book in preference to the print book if both are available. In countries in other parts of the world librarians are acquiring content in digital collections for the first time: i.e., they have never possessed the print versions.

In the Anglophone countries and Europe, some libraries are also replacing print collections with e-books, though others have a policy of not duplicating acquisition of the same publication. This means that if the library already has the print version, it will not purchase the e-book as well. Librarians hit by budget cuts or simply by the erosion of their purchasing power in real terms frequently say that they will cut down on print purchases and/ or invest more in electronic publications. Some are, however, also saying that they no longer have the budget to subscribe to new online collections unless they cancel some of their existing subscriptions; and almost all librarians now take a keen interest in usage statistics as the key indicator of whether they are obtaining 'value for money'. Publishers and aggregators are addressing these issues by providing comprehensive on-site and/ or on-line training for library staff and sophisticated 'customisable' user guides and marketing materials for their patrons, in order to maximise exposure to the e-book collections; and by offering preferential prices for multi-year deals.

The market for academic e-books in the English language also flourishes in other parts of the world, notably in South-East Asia, the Scandinavian and Nordic countries, the Middle East, the more northerly Western European countries, and, to a certain extent, South America. Librarians in Southern Western European and Eastern European countries are also beginning to purchase e-books, though collections in the English language are often not heavily used by their patrons, and they will therefore expect a discount that reflects this. To counteract this, some e-book aggregators now offer certain titles in several different languages.

Discounts reflecting their economic status are expected in any case by 'second world' countries. This can be tricky for publishers, as the economic status of some former Eastern bloc and South-East Asian countries is improving very rapidly. The publisher therefore needs to be careful not to trap itself with over-generous multi-year discounts to library customers in these countries. Even if this is avoided, 'negotiating upwards' – i.e., demanding a higher price when collections are due for renewal – can be tricky. Publishers who have carried out such negotiations successfully advise that offering something additional – such as an archive collection or simultaneous access to more users – is the most effective way of achieving a mutually satisfactory outcome.

'Third world' countries are not significant purchasers of electronic book collections, though some libraries in African countries have shown an interest in them, and certain publishers have responded by selling at highly discounted rates. Sometimes these libraries are the recipients of 'grants' or cash aid from philanthropic trusts, such as the George Soros Foundation, or from benefactor country governments. The Scandinavian countries have a particularly strong tradition of offering this type of aid to Africa. Publishers prepared to discount to poorer countries often therefore find themselves negotiating with third parties. The World Bank will supply a suggested 'sliding scale' of discounts reflecting national purchasing power.

For publishers, the most efficient way of approaching libraries is through consortia. Most libraries belong to one or more consortia, though some, particularly the most prestigious ones with the largest budgets, will still want to do deals independently either instead of or as well as working through a consortium. A list of the key library purchasing consortia worldwide, with contact details, is given in Part Three. When asked what they most want from publishers, academic librarians are likely to mention two things: more electronic textbooks and more 'flexible' pricing. Academics will add 're-purposeable content' to the list.

1.10.3 The student textbook market

Understandably, publishers are reluctant to jeopardise what has hitherto been a successful market – the sale of multiple copies of the same title to, on average, two thirds of the first-year students taking each university course or module – by supplying these titles in e-book format  to academic libraries. However, in recent times a number of factors have come into play that have caused some to re-evaluate their position on e-textbooks. First of all, print textbook sales are declining. There is no single simple reason for this: it has been caused by a complicated mixture of demographic,social and economic changes within the student population, accompanied by shifts in academics' pedagogical approach. The latter have been brought about partly by semesterisation, partly by the need to differentiate courses more clearly from similar courses run by other universities, and partly by the increasingly widespread use of VLEs,individual tutors' websites, and informal teaching methods inspired by Web 2.0 technologies. Instead of letting textbooks continue to wither on the vine, therefore, publishers are more prepared to consider offering them to libraries in the format that they prefer.

In the USA, CourseSmart[49], a joint venture owned by a group of publishers, goes some way to addressing the e-textbook issue. The CourseSmart platform facilitates three types of transaction: it enables publishers to send 'digital comps', or free e-book inspection copies, to academics; it enables students to purchase e-textbooks direct from its website; and it enables the sale of e-textbooks via nominated third parties, such as campus booksellers (though this facility is relatively little used). It does not make e-textbooks available to libraries, thus safeguarding the publishers' revenues from student sales. From the academic's point of view, the main

49 www.coursesmart.com

advantage of such a platform is that the publications hosted are not from one publishing house only, but include textbooks from a wide group of publishers; the platform therefore operates as a one-stop shop. The publisher benefits because the platform acts as a shop window for its publications, and, importantly, because it enables considerable savings to be made by substituting electronic for print inspection copies. Students benefit from being able to take advantage of a quick and easy way to buy or licence the textbooks that they need, and sometimes from the offer of discounts.

In the UK, some publishers are experimenting with making digital comps available via their own websites. Commercial aggregators – e.g., Vital Source and EBook Corporation – are also testing the market by developing e-textbook initiatives.

Whether or not to supply e-textbooks to libraries remains a thorny problem for publishers to have to address. In the UK, a catalyst has been the JISC e-books observatory project, in which 36 course textbooks were made available to UK academic libraries in e-format in return for a premium price, paid for by JISC, reflecting the putative commercial value of the texts on a per-institution basis.[50]

Publishers conducting their own library surveys have discovered that librarians say that they would be prepared to pay similar premiums from their own budgets if publishers would make e-textbooks available. Some publishers who have experimented with the concept have also reported that, instead of jeopardising print sales, e-textbooks can actually help to stimulate them.

1.11   Business models

Partly because the early one-book, one user, outright sale price-plus business model was not attractive to librarians, and partly because in recent years publishers have tried to find ways of pricing e-books that sever the connection with the print price, e-book business models for the institutional market have proliferated. In some ways this has been helpful, because it has offered librarians the variety of choice that they have

---

50 See www.jiscebooksproject.org/the-e-books.

requested; however, they are now being offered so much choice that this has also resulted in confusion and a perception that the acquisition of e-books has become over-complicated.

In the closing years of this decade, more pressure has been put on publishers as library budgets have become squeezed. The rise of the consumer market has also had a significant influence in driving down prices. As outlined in the introduction, there is an increasing expectation that e-books will be 'free' or very cheap, and while publishers are not necessarily obliged to capitulate to this, many trade publishers have recognised that some kind of electronic giveaway – a taster, a chapter, access to a chat-room to 'meet' the author, a game – is required to stimulate sales.

It may be helpful to keep these social and economic contexts in mind when reading the next section.

1.11.1 Main e-book pricing models

There follows a description of the main e-book pricing models. Many minor variations on these also exist.

Cheap or free

- The user is given completely **free access to some or all of the publisher's e-books**. The publisher depends on the user constituency to buy print where appropriate and has taken the decision to provide e-content free. Example: OECD publications.

- The user is given completely **free access to an online collection,** for philanthropic reasons. Example: PubMed.

- Google Books. The user gets **free access to all or part of the content,** depending on whether or not the title is in copyright.

- The user gets **access to online support materials provided free of charge,** usually for a limited period of time, upon purchase of the print volume. This model is frequently used by the big textbook publishers.

- The user gets a **free inspection copy ('sample' or 'digital comp')**, either for access online only or as a download. Usually this facility is only available to academics considering the title for adoption. These free e-books are normally supplied on a case-by-case basis – i.e., the publisher knows the identity of the applicant.

- The **user can avail himself or herself of a Search Inside The Book (SITB) widget,** as pioneered by Amazon. Both trade and academic publishers now make extensive use of the widget. It allows free access to part of the book as a 'taster', or sometimes the whole book if the facility is being used to provide a review copy or as part of a sampling plan – see point above.

- The **user buys a hardware device** which has been pre-loaded with some 'free' publications. These may be included in the price of the device, but some kind of transaction will have taken place between the publisher and the hardware company.

- **Open Access.** This makes the publication free at the point of use, usually to a library[51], sometimes direct to an end-user. Currently it is mainly used for journals; but some book publishers are now experimenting with the O/A model. Example: University of Amsterdam Press.

- **Some online testing suites and resource banks are supplied free** of charge. Example: CUP's Connect Arcade and Interchange Arcade.

- It has already been mentioned in the Introduction that as publishers engage in more e-publishing, they understand the need to engage with their customers and authors direct. Some publishers have now developed **sophisticated online communities, book clubs, chat rooms and collaborative resources.** Examples: Penguin, Palgrave Macmillan, the Royal Society of Chemistry.

---

51 It is free to the library as content provider; but if the author belongs to the same institution as the library, the library may also have been the funds provider.

By annual site licence

Site licences are usually negotiated with libraries and some corporates. Negotiations with academic libraries are sometimes carried out directly between the publisher or aggregator and the library, or, more frequently, between the publisher or aggregator and the consortium to which the library belongs. Sometimes the publisher is represented by a third party such as a subscription agent. Very large organisations such as the NHS have their own procurement departments[52]. There are many possible subtle variations to the models described in below.

- An annual subscription is paid **based on the number of FTEs attending the institution**, which allows unlimited simultaneous usage. Example: The Springer e-books collection.

- An annual subscription is **calculated by counting the relevant number of FTEs attending the institution** – e.g., a subscription to Ovid would be calculated on the basis of the numbers of students, lecturers and researchers studying or teaching Medicine and Health Sciences. From the librarian's perspective, how reasonable this is depends on the breadth of subject matter covered by the product.

- An annual subscription is **based on the number of FTEs and number of concurrent users required.** Example: Lexis Nexis.

- An annual subscription is **calculated according to the number of FTEs and 'research intensity'** that the institution demonstrates (based on an algorithm which takes usage into account). Example: Springer Protocols.

- An annual subscription is calculated **based on the size and type of institution** rather than on FTEs. This is often applied to products that are relevant to all users. Example: 'middleware' products such as Scopus.

52 In the NHS, three types of purchase are made: of general products, for hospitals across the whole organisation; of products for an individual region, which provide resources for the broader but not universal interests specific to that region; and on a single hospital or even single research unit basis, to resource very specialised interests.

- The annual subscription is **based on what the institution can afford**. The existing JISC bandings go some way to achieving this. Applying the same premise, publishers commonly offer large discounts to 'second' and 'third' world countries, sometimes using criteria drawn up by the World Bank or the OECD (though countries can move from 'third' to 'second' world and 'second' to 'first' world with considerable rapidity, which leaves the publisher in the unenviable position of needing to hike the price).

These models can be applied to whole collections or sub-collections.

Many publishers operating site licences offer discounts or guarantee not to raise annual fees beyond an agreed percentage in return for multi-year. commitments from the institution.

Licences to consortia are supplied on a similar basis to the licence models described above, but usually with significantly better pro rata pricing and sometimes other concessions as well.

By outright sale

- Most consumer e-book transactions, whether via the publisher's website, an aggregator's website (such as that of ebooks.com) or via an online bookseller (e.g., Amazon, Blackwell, Waterstone's) are made on an outright sale basis. **Usually the price bears some relationship to the print price**: it might variously be set at parity with paperback or hardback, or calculated as an 'e-price' at somewhere between the two. Some publishers take the hit on VAT, thus ensuring that the e-book is not more expensive than the print version. Some retailers – e.g., Amazon – have sought to drive the price of the e-book down by selling at a uniform price – e.g., US$9.99. The most recent wave of handheld readers has encouraged this approach. E-textbooks delivered either online or offline can be purchased by individual students through the e-textbook aggregators mentioned above (VitalSource, EBooks Corporation and, in North America, CourseSmart), as well as direct from some publishers' websites. These are protected by DRM so that no file-sharing can take place.

- **The 'agency sales' model.** This is a variation on the outright sale model, and was first promoted by Apple earlier this year. The agency model is based on the idea that the publisher is selling to the consumer and, therefore, setting the price, and any 'agent' – usually but not necessarily a retailer - that carries out the actual sales transaction will get a 'commission' from the publisher for doing so. Since Apple's normal 'take' at the App Store is 30 per cent and discounts from publishers have normally been 50 per cent off the established retail price, publishers can claw back margin even if they do not get Apple to concede anything from the 30 per cent. (There has been a great deal of excitement about this, but basically it re-establishes for e-books the principle of Resale Price Maintenance that was the linchpin of the Net Book Agreement. It may therefore come under the scrutiny of government trading departments.)

- Monographs may be sold to an institution in the following ways: by outright **sale on a book-by-book basis,** as part of a complete collection, or as part of a sub-collection. Pricing models vary. They may be set at parity with print, print times 2, 3, 4 or 5, or the print price plus a certain percentage: e.g., NetLibrary often prices at print plus 33 per cent. Whether or not unlimited simultaneous user access is allowed may also be a factor.

- A suitable model has yet to be found for supplying e-textbooks to the institution's library. The recent JISC e-textbook experiment allowed the publishers to charge JISC the **sum total of print textbook sales that they had achieved per institution** in the year before the experiment took place.

- Some publishers have carried out extensive digitisation of backlists, and then **sell the digitised archive that results to institutions as a one-off purchase.** This can be a very lucrative source of income. The price charged may bear some relation to the aggregated print prices of the titles included in the archive, though this is obviously not practicable if they have been out-of-print for a considerable time.

- **Discounts may be offered** on sales of complete collections, sub-collections or bulk pick and mix purchases to institutions. Conversely, there is usually a minimum spend or minimum title purchase requirement for outright sale collections.

- When outright sales of collections have taken place, the publisher or aggregator will charge an **annual maintenance fee** for the platform. This is often waived if the library keeps on adding new purchases to the platform each year.

Hybrid models

- **The 'slot' model.** This was perfected by Safari Techbooks Online. The institution chooses a collection to licence, and at the end of a specified period of time (usually one year) can elect to substitute some of the titles for other titles. As long as the total number of titles in the collection remains constant, the swap does not attract an additional fee. Obviously it works especially well for computer books (the core of the Safari Tech collection), because they date quickly.

- **A collection can be licensed** for a specified number of years, leading to outright sale. One of the e-book models offered by Wiley Interscience operates on this basis. The Wiley model incorporates a further refinement by pairing this with a 'slot' model.

- **Pick-and-mix.** The library chooses the titles, on a minimum purchase basis, and gains access either via subscription or outright purchase.

- **Multi-product platforms.** Journals and e-books and/or pictures and other media may be offered on the same platform. Surprisingly, relatively few publishers have developed this so far, often because the internal structure of their companies has made it difficult to bring about. Example: de Gruyter, using the Atypon platform. Some of the aggregators have pioneered multi-media collections – e.g., NetLibrary, eBrary.

- The publisher may create a **single offer for either the print or e-book,** allowing the customer to choose from the website. de Gruyter once more provides an example. The de Gruyter offer includes 'retro-digitisation' : this means that if the customer requires an e-book of a title that has not already been digitised, de Gruyter undertakes to make it available. The lead time is about ten weeks.

- **"Bundling".** This involves selling the print book and the e-book of the same title/edition together as a single package. The rationale – which is supported by consumer research – is that people like to read books in different formats in different circumstances.

- **Patron Select models.** Several of these have been developed, each one slightly different from the other. They have the same basic characteristics in common: essentially, the library pays a significant sum of money upfront to the publisher or aggregator – typically in the £20,000 - £30,000 range – and the publisher or aggregator makes a substantial collection of e-books available to the library from its catalogue – typically to the value of 5 or 6 times the sum invested. The library can profile these e-books to exclude ones that do not match its selection policies. The e-books appear in the library's catalogue as if the library had purchased them. They can be accessed 'free' for a certain number of times – typically, between two and four times. If they are accessed again after the agreed figure has been reached, the library is deemed to have purchased them, and the relevant sum is deducted from the upfront payment. Various other safeguards are put in place – for example, the library may stipulate that only a certain sum can be spent each month. The model has been widely used in the USA and experimented with in the UK. Broadly speaking, it is considered to be a success, because although the price per use tends to be higher than for books selected by the library, it saves the library many hours that would otherwise be spent on selection time, and is therefore felt to be cost-effective as well as relevant to user needs. MyiLibrary, Springer and EBooks Corporation are among the companies offering this model.

Micro models

Much has been written about micro-models over the past year, though publishers who have implemented them say that to date sales have not been high. However, sales of chapters and part books, or do-it-yourself books incorporating several chapters from different books from the same publisher, have been increasing in the student market recently, and the recent proliferation of e-readers and smartphones is likely to act as a further catalyst.

- **Pay-per-view.** The name aptly describes the model. It was the earliest of the micro-models to appear, originally offered by aggregators, and has been available almost as long as commercially-available e-books. Initially it was aimed at the institutional market, but is now available in the retail sector as well. For several years it was unpopular with librarians, because they believed that it made budget control too difficult. However, with the advent of intelligible COUNTER-compliant usage statistics for e-books, they have come to realise that the pay-per-view economics works better for them than making outright purchases when researchers wish to consult obscure titles that are not in general demand. Librarians have also learnt how to manage their budgets in a more flexible way – see also the Patron Select note in section above.

- **'Chapterisation'.** The premise underpinning this concept is that the reader may want to consult only one or a few chapters in a book, and therefore should not have to pay for the whole volume. However, usually a premium price is charged for the e-chapter. Thus if a book has ten chapters and costs £40, when sold on a per chapter basis, the price might be £8, or double the pro rata cost of the chapter if bought as part of the whole book. However, if the book is not considered to be very popular, the publisher may also discount the chapters.

- **Coursepacks (custom publishing).** The terms 'coursepack' and 'custom publishing' are used interchangeably by some publishers, while to others the term 'coursepack' means the digital copying allowed under the terms of the CLA's digital licence (which permits limited copying from titles selected from across the whole catalogue[53] of participating publishers), and 'custom publishing' means allowing the creation of 'do-it-yourself' textbooks (using only the individual publisher's titles). Some publishers allow subscribers to their e-book collections to create coursepacks at no additional charge, subject to the restrictions imposed by their print/download rules. 'Proper' custom publishing involves allowing an institution to create a publication tailored to the requirements of a particular course by selecting material from several of the publisher's titles. The end result may be supplied either in print or electronically. In return, the institution guarantees an agreed number of sales at an agreed price. McGraw-Hill pioneered this model with Primis.

- **Slice-and-dice** (of chunks of text smaller than chapters); micro-sales (of diagrams, illustrations, etc.). Some academics have expressed warm approval of micro-sales of this nature, because they chime with the concept of 'repurposable learning objects'. Several publishers have experimented with them, despite the associated administrative problems of how to charge a price that makes the work involved worthwhile and how to assign royalties. The question of rights for small published items, particularly diagrams and pictures, is one that is likely to become more important in the future. Publishers are already finding that one of the key obstacles to digitisation is obtaining permission to reproduce digitally the illustrations which feature in the print version of a title[54].

- **Book rental and online collection rental**. Rental allows a longer period of access than pay-per-view, but is still time-limited (and therefore cheaper than outright purchase or an annual licence fee). As with pay-per-view, the pro rata payment is usually more expensive than the other options. Book rental typically lasts for a period of between one week and one month (though online

---

53 Though the publishers are allowed to exclude permission to use certain named titles, and on occasion may do so.
54 Companies have now been set up to trade in these micro-commodities – for example, MediaSelectors and The Licensing Agency.

textbook access via companies like VitalSource is typically for one semester or one year).

Emerging models

The following ideas or suggestions have been expressed in recent discussion fora:

- Disaggregated online collections.

- Country-wide or international licences for big digital projects (such as ARROW and Europeana).

- Retail subscription models.

- Custom publishing via 'neutral' third parties such as RROs.

- More free or very cheap starter offers in both the retail and institutional sector, to try to gain customer loyalty – cf. traditional book clubs.

1.11.2 The main business models in more detail

It will be apparent from the above that four main models are responsible for generating publishers' revenues. These are described in more detail below.

The retail model

This works as follows:

- The **end-user buys a discrete copy of the e-book direct through the publisher's or bookseller's website;** or alternatively has bought a device pre-loaded with a selection of e-books, either paid for with 'tokens', or included within the price of the device itself.

- Publishers and booksellers often use a **'prefabricated electronic retail service'** – e.g., Taylor and Francis uses Value Chain's ebookstore; W.H. Smith uses OverDrive's ContentReserve.

- Some publishers offer refinements on the purchase of the whole book: for example, Taylor & Francis offers 'eCompile', which allows students to select chapters from different titles to create a do-it-yourself publication.

- Now that e-books can be downloaded on to mobile phones and more sophisticated e-book readers are available, some publishers are experimenting with a **retail subscription model**. Harlequin, Mills and Boon[55] is a successful pioneer of this concept. It offers a regular supply of e-book titles to readers on a subscription basis, 'bundled' packages of several titles at cut-price rates, and free e-reads from its website. Academic and educational publishers have watched this development with interest, understanding that the model holds possibilities for their student market. Academic publishers also offer 'taster' facilities – for example, the opportunity either to view certain pages of the text free of charge, or gain access to the full text for a limited period of time (say, 20 minutes) before the service 'times out'. 'Tasters' have gained prominence with the advent of the widget, or 'search inside the book' (SITB) facility. This will be considered in more detail in the next section.

- Working on the Google principle, some publishers are taking the audacious step of **making the 'penny plain' digitised version of the book available completely free of charge**. Bloomsbury Academic[56] has experimented with this model, arguing that most readers will be prepared to pay either for a 'better' version of the e-text with more enhanced functionality, or for the print book.

---

55   See www.millsandboon.co.uk
56   www.bloomsburyacademic.com/news.htm

The institutional business model (1): the direct sale library model

- The library 'buys' a copy of the book 'in perpetuity', either direct from the publisher or from an aggregator.

- If sold through an aggregator, the price charged is usually agreed with the publisher. Unless it is a textbook, the **price usually bears some relationship to the print version**. Some aggregators charge more for the e-book than print.

- **Aggregators commonly charge a 'maintenance fee'** for the platform itself. This is not shared with the publisher.

- The advantage of the model is that, historically, librarians have said that they prefer to 'own' the book (though some are revising their thinking on this). For the publisher, it **counts as a direct sale** (meaning that the author royalty is a standard 10 per cent). From the publisher's point of view, it works just like a print book sale, meaning that the library has to buy the next edition when it comes out, and extra copies if more than one reader wants to access it at the same time – unless the library has paid a premium for multi-user access.

The institutional business model (2): the subscription model

- The library buys access to a collection by paying for an **annual subscription**, or licence, either to the publisher or to an aggregator.

- **Prices are set according to the subject area and the number of titles offered**, and usually based on the number of FTE equivalents using the library, or the number of FTE equivalents likely to be interested in the subject(s), if this can be determined and agreed upon. Subject collections may be off-the-shelf – i.e., pre-selected by the publisher – or 'bespoke' by the library, i.e., chosen on a book-by-book basis by the library. 'Bespoke' collections were allowed by publishers in response to librarian requests for more control over the titles making up the collection.

However, publishers report that in practice the publishers' own collections are more frequently licensed.

- Various refinements to this model have been developed. For example, **some publishers or aggregators will offer a discount** or promise to hold the licence fee unaltered if a multi-year deal is agreed. Sometimes an agreement is reached with the library that it has purchased the collection outright after having paid the licence fee for a stipulated number of years - though it would not be entitled to any new editions of the titles under this arrangement. Sometimes 'slot' models are offered, in which the library agrees to a multi-year licence and chooses a collection of titles in the first year which it can then change on a title-by-title basis, according to demand, in subsequent years. If the 'slot' model is being operated in tandem with a multi-year licence leading to outright purchase, titles substituted after the first year will not be deemed to have been 'purchased' until they have been licensed for the requisite number of years. Although publishers have developed this model with the intention of giving librarians more flexibility over title control and 'ownership', it is complex and time-consuming to administer, and can lead to misunderstandings.

- The advantage to publishers and other vendors of licensing models, even the ones that lead to ultimate purchase, is that the publisher gets an **assured repeating chunk of income over a number of years** (unless, of course, the library cancels the subscription). The disadvantage is that librarians often dislike subscriptions because they feel that they have 'nothing to show for them, and instinctively prefer outright purchase. They are also suspicious of prices based on 'notional' value, rather than the 'transparency' of the relationship of individual e-book prices to print prices. To counteract this, some publishers will provide librarians with detailed calculations to show how they arrived at the price being asked.

- Since the **cost of a licence for one year is usually lower than purchasing the same collection outright**, if the publisher or aggregator offers both outright sale and licensing models, librarians will often choose to licence first, in order to ascertain how popular the collection will be, and then purchase outright if usage statistics merit.

The institutional business model (3): book rental, micro-purchase, do it-yourself custom titles

- The library or individual can visit the aggregator's or the publisher's website and rent access to a title for a limited time; buy individual chapters of the title; or combine several chapters from different publications to create a 'do-it-yourself' customised text.

- Librarians disliked these 'pay-as-you go' models when they were first introduced, because they felt that they were time-consuming and also caused difficulties with budget management. However, they are now realising that they offer the most economical way of providing information to students who want material outside the mainstream, and to researchers who are most likely to want to use the publications during the months of the summer vacation. The models have, of course, become much more familiar as retail e-book sales have increased.

1.12   Digital Rights Management (DRM)

Digital Rights Management is the term commonly used to refer to access control technologies that can be used by hardware manufacturers, publishers, copyright holders and individuals to try to impose limitations on the usage of digital content and devices.   DRM technologies have enabled publishers to enforce access policies that not only disallow copyright infringements, but also implement use constraints on works that they have digitised in certain formats, whether or not they hold the copyright.

The use of DRM is therefore controversial. Those in favour of it maintain that it is essential to prevent file-sharing or other unauthorised duplication of publications likely to result in erosion of sales. Those against it assert that copyright holders are attempting to restrict use of copyrighted material in ways not covered by existing laws, or that use of proprietary DRM products directly or indirectly results in anti-competitive practices[57].

When the first aggregated collections of e-books were created, DRM was essential, because publishers would not make their publications available to aggregators who did not have a DRM application in place. It is fair to say that most publishers would still not make their e-books available without DRM on aggregated platforms. However, some are beginning to experiment with not using it on their own platforms. One of the factors influencing this is the marked dislike for DRM applications shown by retail consumers, particularly the fact that DRM locks them in to buying files in formats suitable for only one device, when they might, for example, wish to read the same e-book at different times on a PC or a hand-held reader or a mobile phone. Another aspect of some DRM applications which annoys end-users is that they can only be viewed on a page-by-page basis.

Some publishers are prepared to allow file-sharing, and have never used DRM. An example is the OECD's publications division[58]. The OECD argues that most of its clients are honourable enough not to indulge in illegal file-sharing; but that even if they do, such activities just help to promote sales of both print and electronic books, and therefore are not detrimental in the long run. Springer has removed DRM from its e-books and is making positive use of this decision by experimenting with on-demand POD versions of all its (approximately 11,500) digitised titles[59].

Some of the off-the-shelf e-book platforms available – for example, IngentaConnect – do not operate a DRM system. Publishers or aggregators who license cross-searchable e-book collections, especially if they are not in PDF format, have little to fear from file-sharing.

---

57   That Amazon only allows downloads via Mobipocket, a company which it acquired in 2005, is
       often cited to prove this point
58   See www.oecd.org/publications/0,3353,en_2649_201185_1_1_1_1_1,00.html
59   See http://speaking.stanford.edu/library/Print_Springer_EBooks.html

A more user-friendly option is digital watermarking. This does not actually prevent abuse of copyright or file-sharing, but acts as a deterrent because it makes obvious any contravention of terms. It is the process of irreversibly embedding information into a digital signal. The signal may be delivered via audio, pictures (including text) or video. If the signal is copied, then the information is also carried in the copy. With visible watermarking, the information is visible in the picture or video. Typically, the information is some text or a logo which identifies the owner of the media. With invisible watermarking, the information is added as digital data but cannot be perceived as such, although it is still possible to detect it.

It is for the individual publisher to decide whether or not to use some form of DRM or watermarking. To a large extent, this will depend on the type of publication being digitised, and the types of market that the publisher is trying to attract. There is no one-size-fits-all answer.

1.13 Secure access

Many libraries wish to use a secure single online access product to ensure that their online resources are only being used by authorised patrons. This is clearly also in the publisher's interest, especially if the price of its licence has been based on FTE equivalents.

Traditionally, libraries in the UK and sometimes in Europe have favoured Athens, which is owned by Eduserv. Its features include:

- secure single sign-on access to multiple web-based services
- devolved administration facilities at organisation level
- remote access user accounts
- encrypted bulk user-account upload services
- the ability to support millions of user accounts
- resilient architecture.

Publishers and aggregators are charged a (relatively small) annual subscription fee to adopt Athens. At present, subscribing to it constitutes a 'hygiene factor' for doing business with many libraries; however, the more forward-looking libraries are already experimenting with Shibboleth, which adopts a more international approach to access. Athens has now developed two versions of the access product, Classic Athens (the original) and Open Athens, a federated system[60].

Shibboleth is proving to be a more internationally successful access system than Athens. It is emerging as the system of choice for most of the US, and in several European countries and Australia. It is now being experimented with by some UK HEIs, and Athens/Shibboleth interoperability has been developed by Eduserv[61].

1.14   Royalties

Most publishers have now changed their author contracts so that they also cover electronic rights; and although there has been no proper survey undertaken on electronic royalties, when asked most publishers say that they pay the same royalty percentage for electronic publications as for print. There has been some resistance to this from a minority of authors.

Once electronic rights are included in the standard contract, problems arising for publishers with e-book royalties may include:

- **Getting authors to agree to issue backlist titles not covered by the contract in e-book format.** In practice, however, authors are unlikely to object, especially if this represents a way of keeping the book in print.

- **Agreeing and administering a split of royalties for multi-author works.** This, of course, is also a problem with print books; and it becomes more complicated with e-books when a licensing model, rather than a straightforward selling model, is used.

60   www.athensams.net/federations/openathens.aspx
61   See www.shibboleth.lnternet2.edu and www.athensams.net/shibboleth

- **Complications for the publisher if it does not hold world rights** to the title – since by their nature e-books can easily be supplied to anywhere in the world. Agreements with aggregators, etc. can specify that e-books will only be supplied to certain territories; but enforcing this in practice may be difficult – though most aggregators and DAM companies now have sophisticated systems in place that diminish the risks.

The Society of Authors' 'Guide to Publishing Contracts[62]' (2009) states:

> "On e-books and download audiobooks, we believe the author should receive at least 25 per cent (royalties), preferably 35 per cent, rising at an agreed level of sales. Some publishers offer 50 per cent of net receipts, most others offer 15 -25 per cent. Resist anything less than that."[63]

The Society of Authors also recommends that authors should ask for between 50 and 80 per cent of 'sub-licensed e-book rights'. Some publishers have interpreted this to include e-books sold through aggregators, sometimes resulting in their refusal to work with aggregators or other third parties. However, the Guide does say that authors of scholarly, professional and educational works should expect royalties of 10–15 per cent.

On the whole, trade authors have expressed more concern about the extremely low prices at which some trade e-books are being sold than about royalties per se. Academic monograph authors have so far mostly been receptive to the idea of their work being available in e-book format, because they publish primarily for reputation and to build their careers, rather than for the revenue that they make. However, textbook authors,who are generally much more interested in the income that they make from writing, have not really been put to the test yet: as has already

---

62 See www.societyofauthors.org/guides-and-articles
63 This advice is given on the premise that 'many of the publishers traditional costs do not apply' to e-books and audiobooks. However, as this manual explains elsewhere, e-books are often not significantly cheaper to produce than print books – and may even be more expensive, if the publisher takes the hit on VAT; and audiobooks are often more expensive to produce than print by a factor of several hundred per cent.

been mentioned, publishers are still very wary about making textbooks available in e-format. Over the past two years, also as mentioned earlier, there have been significant experiments undertaken with e-textbooks within the academic library community. There may be good reasons for publishers to change their attitude to e-textbooks in the future; in addition, enabling digital 'slicing-and-dicing' and 'chunking' of textbook material may present both publishers and authors with opportunities that are perceived to be less of a threat.

1.15   Conversion companies and DAM companies

Conversion is rapidly becoming a commodity process, and for this reason the most established conversion companies are searching for ways to differentiate themselves. They may, for example, suggest ways of adding  value to the publisher's 'back-end' processes, such as copy-editing, or offer an end-to-end typesetting service from which the e-book 'drops out' as part of the procedure. The most advanced are developing Digital Asset Management (DAM) systems, which take a new approach to the e-book supply chain, and emphasise both their content repurposing capabilities, and the security of their hosting system. Such companies may not charge for the conversion process at all, but recoup their costs from the hosting/ warehousing charges which form the basis of their price schedules.

Most but not all conversion companies operate 'offshore' – typically in India, elsewhere in South-East Asia, the Philippines or China. Some publishers are wary of placing conversion work in China at present because the quality of the product is often not acceptable, though this is likely to change. Chinese conversion services are usually the cheapest. Conversion work is also done in Eastern Europe, the UK and the US. Despite its commodity nature, the prices charged vary greatly, and the offshore countries are not always the cheapest. As well as obviously being caused by the differing costs of living and workplace standards between the countries in which the work is carried out (which in their turn may raise ethical considerations before publishers commit to working with certain contractors), the price discrepancies are also the result of the conversion company's approach to its business: i.e., whether it chooses to operate by throwing people at projects, or by investing in sophisticated technology. US and UK publishers often take steps to establish that the working practices of offshore companies are ethical – i.e., that they are not running 'sweatshops'.

The following sections describe briefly some of the best-known conversion companies currently working for US and UK publishers (companies completely owned by the publishers themselves, such as Thomson Digital, have not been included). Most of these companies can digitise content in multiple formats: for Print on Demand, e-books, audiobooks, DVD, sometimes music, etc. Most now offer DAM systems and some offer other services, such as 'back-end' editorial suites and marketing solutions.

1.15.1 Aptara[64]

Aptara is the name given to the company formerly known as 'Techbooks'. For a long time, Techbooks was the market leader in content conversion. It now markets its services in four groups: Digital Publishing Solutions, Editorial and Composition Services, Content Technology Solutions and Learning and Performance Solutions, and emphasises its prowess at repurposing content as text, audio or video. It is a large company, with more than 300 customers and 3,700 employees, and has offices in many countries, including the USA, the UK and Australia. Its main production facilities are situated at two locations in India. Its charges are perceived to be competitive, though not the cheapest.

1.15.2 Atypon[65]

Atypon is a well-established American company with a fully operational UK office. It says that it works closely with publishers to establish their future needs, create solutions, and deliver them at an affordable cost.

---

64 www.aptaracorp.com
65 www.atypon.com

Its clients are typically small to medium academic or learned society publishers, though it has some large publisher clients as well. In the past, the emphasis of its work has been on hosting electronic journals, but it has now successfully entered the e-book sector.

Atypon offers a number of services:

- **Atypon Premium** is a fully hosted e-publishing solution for clients who wish to manage the entire process of delivering and managing their content online. Publishers have direct control over all stages of content production, linking and depositing, as well as access rights and multi-level business model provision.

- **Atypon Link** provides a cost-effective, aggregated hosting and delivery platform for publishers who prefer a fully outsourced e-publishing service.

- **eRights Suite**, which includes Right Access and Right Commerce.

1.15.3 codeMantra[66]

In recent years codeMantra has gradually gained a reputation for the quality of its conversion services, and is often favoured by e-book aggregators. For clients not willing to incur the cost of XML conversion, codeMantra has developed a product called the 'Universal PDF', which provides high-quality text with some search capability. codeMantra offers a matrix pricing structure, from which publishers can choose any suite of services from PDF to PDF + POD to ePub to full XML. The Universal PDF + POD solution is the most popular, and prices for it are competitive. The full XML suite is expensive (more expensive than that of some of codeMantra's competitors), but it is generally agreed by publishers that the ePub version covers most needs. This is appreciably cheaper. Conversion work is carried out in India. codeMantra has developed Collection Point, a basic DAM solution, which is charged for separately from the conversion service on a per-title-hosted-per-year basis. Discounts per title are offered at various volume break-points.

66   www.codeMantra.com

1.15.4 Content Data Services (formerly Thomas Technologies)[67]

Originating from Philadelphia but with a long-established London office, Content Data Services (CDS), which was called Thomas Technologies until earlier this year, has an impressive list of clients on both sides of the Atlantic, including a strong mainland-European customer base. Its solutions are bespoke. They are relatively cheap as bespoke systems go. CDS offers a stage-by-stage payment process. Publishers can pay a proportion of the costs upfront and the remainder after the platform has been launched and starts earning revenues. Ongoing maintenance is typically 15 per cent of the set-up cost. Where appropriate, platforms that it has developed for previous clients can be offered for adaptation to new customer requirements, typically at less than half the bespoke cost. Development time is lengthy: from six to nine months. The company gives the impression of being safe, solid and tried-and-tested rather than innovative or cutting-edge.

1.15.5 Ingram Content Companies[68]

Ingram Digital's CoreSource is a digital asset warehousing and distribution product. It is a modular service, involving a suite of products from which publishers can choose the following: conversion (to ePub, PDF, Quark, POD, MP3, MPEG or XML); an e-content repository; and a Digital Asset Management System. Some publishers report that CoreSource offers good value for money.

There is a 'family' of Ingram Digital products which complement each other. The others include MyiLibrary[69], the aggregated e-book platform (see below); Vital Source[70], the customisable e-book platform for colleges and schools; and Lightning Source[71], the Print on Demand company (see below).

---

67 www.contentdsi.com
68 www.ingrampublisherservices.com/about/learnmore.aspx
69 www.myilibrary.com
70 www.ingramdigital.com/education/students
71 www.lightningsource.com

1.15.6 Innodata-Isogen[72]

Innodata-Isogen is a large company with a good pedigree. It is US-based, with a UK office, and turnover of more than $80m, and it operates several conversion plants, which are situated in the Philippines, Sri Lanka and India. Its core business is 'mark-up language related', which means that its preferred medium is XML, though it will offer PDF conversion as well.

It works in part by developing strategic alliances with other digital companies – for example, Mark Logic and Macmillan Publishing Services. Its work is said by publishers to be of a good standard, though it is more expensive than some conversion companies.

1.15.7 Klopotek[73]

Klopotek has been selling software to the publishing industry since 1992. It adopts a standardised, modular approach to solutions, which may be helpful to publishers seeking to build a fully-integrated system in stages. The company is strong in North America, the UK and Europe. Its long-term experience lies in journals distribution, which means that it has developed workable and sophisticated back-end procedures; it has also been active in e-book distribution for several years. It acts as a reseller for IngentaConnect[74], an off-the-shelf solution often chosen by small academic and learned society publishers.

1.15.8 LibreDigital[75]

LibreDigital is based in Austin, Texas, and has a European office in the UK and also a senior manager based in the UK. Conversion and development work are partly carried out in the US, partly outsourced. LibreDigital offers an integrated Digital Asset Management system, the core features of which it describes as follows: it ingests physical and digital content via a normalised, high-quality process; stores content in a manner that enables access to each object (e.g. image, page, and title); delivers content in Internet appropriate formats at Internet speed; applies rights and

---

72 www.innodata-isogen.com
73 www.klopotek.de/products/enindex.htm
74 www.ingenta.com/corporate/publishers/academic
75 www.libredigital.com

permissions rules for every partner access to every object; displays content in a controlled, secure fashion (e.g. the BookBrowse Flash Reader 'widget': it offers Search Inside the Book functionality); and tracks and reports on all activity. The technology was developed for the online newspaper and magazine industry: LibreDigital grew out of NewsStand. Of all the platform providers, it has perhaps been the most innovative in striking up partnerships with device-makers, which has given it a strong presence in the retail publishing market. It also has some well-known academic publisher clients.

Charging is based on the following: an initial deployment fee, plus conversion fee per title plus a monthly maintenance fee per title, plus 'reflow' upload charges for different e-book formats. 'Widgets' are charged for separately. No commission is charged on content sold – the core revenue stream comes from the monthly maintenance fee. This means that the more successful the publisher is at achieving sales, the more economical the partnership with LibreDigital becomes. LibreDigital is also prepared to negotiate with publishers on revenue share.

There are four key LibreDigital products, which can be purchased separately and together comprise the full solution:

- **BookBrowse,** which is purchased on a book-by-book basis, and is viral—each comes with a BookWidget that allows people who have enjoyed the book to share the browse experience on their own web pages. At the same time, control remains with the publisher, because the latter determines the number of pages in a BookBrowse, how long it is available for each book and how it is connected to points of purchase.

- **iBrowse,** which has established itself as the leading e-solution for newspapers, and has been adapted by LibreDigital to host both scholarly journals and magazines. Online education programmes also use iBrowse.

- **LibreDigital's Digital Warehouse,** which can handle all forms of content—any type of book, newspaper, or journal—and prepare it for delivery in any format, in concordance with the publisher's rights and permissions.

- The **Digital Distribution system**, offered as part of the Digital Warehouse, makes content current: readable and purchasable online, deliverable to any e-reader and handheld device.

1.15.9 Macmillan Publishing Solutions (MPS)[76]

The MPS ebookstore was developed in India, and maintenance and development work is carried out there. Essentially it is an off-the-shelf solution for both retail and B2B customers.   It consists of several 'suites' of solutions: Book Store Discovery (a marketing solution which includes a widget); Book Store Digital (a retail sales solution); Book Store Academic; Book Store Distribution (a DAD, or Digital Asset Distribution system); and Book Store Custom Publishing (a DAM solution). MPS offers a conversion service which converts content in any format to ePub. The model is based on a fixed site build cost plus cumulative annual service and conversion charges which rise as the number of titles increases, but simultaneously reduce on a per title basis: so, for example, the annual cost for a batch of 2,000 titles is cheaper than the annual cost by title for a batch of 1,000 titles.

1.15.10 Mark Logic[77]

Mark Logic is based in the US. It has a UK manager, and is active across Europe and in Canada, as well as the US. Its product was originally developed to serve the US Defense Department. It offers a Rolls-Royce bespoke solution that centres upon the Mark Logic Content Server, and has an impressive client list which includes most of the big academic publishing houses. It describes its solution as "a secure, scalable platform that enables the creation and delivery of highly customised content products, providing all the key characteristics of a high-end database, it delivers performance, scalability and programmability for content similar to what a relational database provides for numeric data". It works almost exclusively in XML. The Content Server exploits enabling technology which is used to build the customised content products – it is not a generic shared or hosted offering.

---

76   www.mpstechnologies.com
77   www.marklogic.com

It has two key USPs: one is that the Mark Logic Server can be used as a 'platform of platforms', to enable different solutions provided by the same publishing house to 'speak' to each other. The other is that the technology can create a complete customised publication 'on the fly', with pagination, chapter headings and even page headings created from, say, individual chapters from 10 different books changed to create a 'new' book in seconds.

From the publisher's point of view, the main downside to working with Mark Logic is that it does not provide an end-to-end solution. It uses a range of partners to provide hosting services, design interfaces, etc. As well as adding to the expense, this may leave the customer unsure about where responsibility lies for each part of the system. The Mark Logic solution is not cheap, but its customers seem to agree that they get what they pay for. Annual maintenance charges are typically c20 per cent of set-up.

1.15.11 MetaPress[78]

MetaPress is an EBSCO company. It is based in the USA, in Birmingham, Alabama, but has a high profile in the UK, and attends UK book fairs and other major publishing events.

MetaPress' one-off charges for providing an electronic platform include development fee, content upload fee and maintenance fee. Thereafter, it is remunerated according to the amount of content loaded. It does not collect a fee for any authorised distribution of the publisher content. If a user decides to purchase content on a pay-per-view basis via the credit card transaction e-commerce facility, then MetaPress will collect a transaction processing charge to cover the cost of credit company fees and administration. Otherwise, MetaPress has no part in the collection of revenue for access.

The publisher maintains control over access rights to all content. Access control is based upon the publisher's sales model and can vary by title which maximises the flexibility accorded to the publisher. Watermarking

---

78 www.metapress.com/home/main.mpx

of each printed page is available; the watermark will contain the identifying information of the authenticated user.

The publisher has complete control of the price and subsequent revenue stream. MetaPress would only receive commission in the event of the user purchasing a book or chapter using the e-commerce facility that is available; otherwise MetaPress collects no fees associated with revenue and has no part in the collection of revenue for access through other sales channels. Pricing models are therefore formulated entirely at the discretion of the publisher. The access control is then configured around the resultant models adopted by the publisher. The MetaPress access control system allows the publisher to group titles into 'bundles' for sale to libraries, library consortia etc. Models include subject-constructed packages and more customised collections that allow the librarian to select titles to create their own package from a pre-defined set of titles.

MetaPress does not sell directly on behalf of any of its clients. It has a sister company, EMpact Sales, that offers tailored marketing and sales activity to publishers.

MetaPress processes online credit card transactions daily and reimburses the publisher with revenues collected less a transaction fee on a monthly basis. The publisher retains complete control of all the other sales channels and revenue streams currently in place. It has no direct compensation requirement for sales and access that is obtained via publisher sales channels.

1.15.12 North Plains[79]

North Plains is a well-established Canadian company which has been offering publishing solutions for about fifteen years, though it is not well-known in the UK. It now offers what it calls an 'end-to end solution', from manuscript, editing and production of the published content and storage and cataloguing of titles and components through to promotion, distribution and sales of content. Titles are securely stored in a flexible format which can be 'reflowed' to PDF, POD, eBook and HTML output as required. Widget technology is also available.

79 www.northplains.com

1.15.13 OverDrive[80]

OverDrive is an interesting company because it offers solutions for each of the main sectors in the electronic publishing supply chain. It was also one of the first companies to understand the potential of e-books, and scored some notable firsts, particularly in retail and in the supply of e-books to public libraries. It offers a distribution service for e-books, digital publications, audiobooks, music, and video. Publishers and booksellers can both use OverDrive's hosting and storage technology to deliver their titles through their own customer-facing website or channels. Though the company is based in the USA, its ContentReserve application reaches thousands of libraries, schools, and retailers worldwide. The key to all of its solutions, whether for publishers, booksellers, commercial companies, libraries or schools, is that they offer an affordable 'white label' product which can be branded and gives the appearance of belonging 'seamlessly' to the organisation itself.

The suite of solutions cannot be described in detail here, but are worth exploring in more detail (see www.overdrive.com/products/publisher.asp). Publishers using OverDrive set the permissions for each title sold and the territorial rights for each edition. If the publisher wishes, these can be set globally, but individual permissions and rights on a title-by-title basis can also be accommodated, as can the addition of region-specific sales tax or VAT, to be levied at the time of purchase. OverDrive supports a number of different pricing models, the most common of which is outright sales on a book-by-book basis, though subscription and membership-style models can also be supported, as well as individual 'one-off' deals. There is sometimes a maintenance charge for the platform.

1.15.14 PubFactory[81]

PubFactory is a mixed-medium online publishing platform developed by iFactory, an American company that began by designing websites. PubFactory was built from inception to support e-books, reference works and journals in a variety of XML formats on the same platform, with support for PDF, images and other media. It offers advanced functionality,

---

80   www.overdrive.com
81   www.pubfactory.net

management tools for librarians and administrators, and a back-end suite that gives the publisher control over content and customer relationship management. It provides publishers with pricing flexibility by supporting a variety of different revenue models, including renewable time-limited subscriptions, one-time purchase with perpetual access, and pay-per-view. Credit card transactions can be accepted by the publisher by using PubFactory's built-in support or an external e-commerce system. Content can be sold in small 'chunks' and free content can be offered from the platform on a time-limited basis.

iFactory's greatest strength lies in the attractive, clear front-end 'skins' it designs for its clients. For this reason it has been chosen by several UK publishers – both trade and academic – recently.

1.15.15 Semantico[82]

Semantico is a relatively small British-based company which has managed to attract some high-profile clients in recent years. It supplies solutions through two core products, Semantico Information Publishing Platform and Semantico Access Management System. The latter is a fairly sophisticated DRM system, not a full DAM system. The platform is at the high end of off-the-shelf – the basic product can be tailored very considerably. The basic platform is said to be 'very competitively' priced.

1.15.16 Siemens[83]

Siemens provides tailored services which range from strategic advice to devising integrated operational and technological solutions and running outsourced IT operations. It has been offering its services to the publishing industry for the past 20 years. Services and solutions include:

- Integration of advertising management and editorial production pre-press solutions, which save production time and enable multi-format publishing

---

82 www.semantico.com/corporate
83 www.siemens.com/media

- Development and launch of web 2.0 based solutions to increase potential for print-based publishers to move into digital markets

- Customer relationship management solution development and deployment to identify new markets and provide quicker responses to customer demand

- 'Back end' management tools for organising customer data and financial reporting

- Implementation of content management solutions

- Provision of IT managed and outsourced services, including web hosting, desktop support and applications management.

1.15.17 SPi Tech[84]

SPi Tech evolved from being a service-provider to publishers for back-end editorial, content production and business processes. It is a large-scale operation with about equal book and journal publishing clientele. It is the 'invisible' hosting partner for several large journals publishers and also offers DAMs. It is jointly owned by holding companies in the US, Singapore and the Philippines. Conversion work is carried out in the US, Philippines and India, and it has offices in the USA and Belgium. It has a good track record for conversion work (XML or PDF), and its prices are said by publishers to be in the medium range.

1.15.18 Value Chain[85]

Value Chain is a company that has changed hands several times. It was formerly Digital Publishing Solutions (DPSL), and prior to that a company called Versaware. At present it is owned by an Indian holding company with registered offices in Australia and Singapore. It has business offices in the USA and the UK. The conversion plants are situated at two locations in India. When it was set up, the company was ahead of its time in that it has always worked with XML, even to convert back into PDF format. The

84   www.spi-bpo.com
85   www.valuechaininc.com

conversion technique that it has developed is extremely cost-effective. Its conversion service has an extensive list of publisher clients, and it provides the hosting solutions for some publishers and wholesalers, including Gardners Books in the UK. It also offers a DAM system.

1.15.19 VirtuSales[86]

VirtuSales is based in Hove in the UK. It works with large publishing houses that operate on both sides of the Atlantic, and also with some publishers that are exclusively US or UK. In what it has described as a 'totally reactive' partnership with several large clients, VirtuSales has developed a product called Biblio which it describes as a "complete publishing system'. Biblio co-ordinates editorial processes, production costings and timeflows, contracts, royalties, bibliographical data and the management of documents and images, and distribution. It is a single database system that manages the total workflow; out of this drops the publishers' assets, including content that can then be repurposed in different formats. For smaller publishers, there is a cheaper version called BiblioLite. It now also offers a DAM system called BiblioDam.

1.16   Choosing a digital partner: the implications

Although the above list is not exhaustive, and space for detail about individual companies is limited, a considerable proportion of this report

has been devoted to supplying information about potential digital partners for publishers, because the choice of partner will have far-reaching consequences as digital solutions companies continue to move beyond 'commodity' conversion work, differentiate their products, and build 'end-to-end' solutions of different kinds. The most sophisticated solutions seek to provide not only a 'cradle to grave' creation and support package for each title, but to enable content to be enhanced or 'repurposed' in

---

86   www.virtusales.com/page.aspx?id=122

many different ways. For trade publishers, this may mean adding an extra dimension to the publication, such as an interactive game. For academic publishers, it may make it possible the use of the same e-content within a variety of different contexts; it also brings them within reach of using the medium to create e-books in more exciting formats than as digital replicas of the printed page, thus better exploiting the technology and 'adding value'.

Publishers therefore need to undertake a complex decision-making process before making their choice. Important issues to address include:

- **Cost** (of course); but if an expensive solution is out of the question, it is important not to choose one that cannot be built on later. A solution sold in modules may therefore be appropriate.

- A solution that **supports XML** is essential, even if the publisher is not contemplating the use of XML in the short term.

- Exactly what is **the premium that customers will be prepared to pay** for 'value added' products? There will certainly be a price point beyond which the customer will not pay, regardless of how much functionality and elegance the end result can offer.

- **How flexible is the proposed digital partner on payment arrangements?** Some will accept an initial payment that represents only a proportion of the total cost, and allow the remainder to be paid via a revenue-share arrangement as the e-books begin to sell. Note: if this type of arrangement appeals, the publisher needs to remember to agree an option to renegotiate the contract once the cost of the platform has been paid for.

- **Geographical location of the digital partner** may be important. Although technologically speaking the solution can be delivered from anywhere, it may be important for the publisher to have appropriate technical back-up close at hand (i.e., a technical support person or team operating in the same country). Technical support by telephone should be available 24x7, to ensure that the working hours of both the publisher and its clients are covered.

- **Proof of concept.** Some digital companies will build 'dummy' systems, utilising some of the publisher's own content, to demonstrate how the solution works. If the publisher wants a detailed build, the digital company may ask for a proof of concept payment which can then be deducted from the final cost of the solution if the publisher chooses to accept it.

- In either the short or long term, is the publisher considering placing **e-books and e-journals on the same platform?** If so, is the platform under consideration suitable for both?

- **Third party partners.** How important is the solution provider's own group of partners – e.g., device manufacturers, channel distributors, possible outsource partners – to the publisher? If some of the technological 'build' is outsourced, is it quite clear with whom the responsibility rests for the different components of the solution, and is the publisher entirely happy with this arrangement, or does it appear to be too fragile or too complex?

- **Administrative systems.** Does the proposed digital partner deliver management information and other statistics in 'real time', so that the same information can be examined by members of the same publishing house working, for example, on either side of the Atlantic? Some companies have very sophisticated 'front end' solutions in which they have invested most of their resource, leaving their 'back end' systems messy and only semi-automated. Most publishers still have only very small digital departments, and therefore not the time or people resources to carry out monotonous and time-consuming tasks such as 'manual' analysis of spreadsheets.

- **'Disaster' management.** What back-up systems does the platform provider have in place to counteract system crashes or other disasters, such as fire or insolvency?

- **Financial robustness.** How financially secure is the platform provider and any possible third-party contributors to the platform 'build'? A stringent due diligence process is essential. Although all of the companies listed in the previous section have been in operation for a number of years, and appear to be robust, this sector is still very volatile; and there are many other, lesser known, companies trying to enter the market, some of which are undoubtedly 'cowboys'.

1.17   New ways of marketing: Web 2.0

A key advantage offered to publishers by electronic platform providers is the opportunity to carry out 'viral marketing', or marketing through the use of Web 2.0 technologies. This is achieved in a number of ways, including through blogs, through 'chat rooms' and listservs, and – an enormously effective development - through the manufacture of a widget that can be dropped into social networks. This marketing tool has been pioneered by trade publishers, with impressively successful results – publishers who have been exploiting widget technology in tandem with social netware for some time claim that it enhances sales by between 7 and 17 per cent.

Web 2.0 is a generic term for a growing range of social netware applications, and is about 'harnessing collective intelligence'. Therefore, hyperlinking is at the heart of its nervous system. "Much as synapses form in the brain, with associations becoming stronger through repetition or intensity, the web of connections grows organically as an output of the collective activity of all web users." A great deal has already been written about Web 2.0, some of it in high-flown pseudo-academic language which can be needlessly confusing and over-complicated. Of more practical use are those websites which attempt to list social networking sites as comprehensively as possible, and which are regularly updated. Traffikd offers an example[87].

Short descriptions are given below of the most popular sites used by authors and publishers to promote themselves and their books.

1.17.1 Facebook[88]

Facebook started life as an academic networking tool, allowing undergraduates and academics to stay in touch with each other. It was

---

87 See http://traffikd.com/social-media-websites
88 www.facebook.com/home.php?

originally used to promote academic publications and events, especially those that served particular interest groups, and of the main social network sites it has the most sophisticated security tools. People join Facebook within one or more networks, and that network excludes people outside it. Therefore institutions use it through a domain name (such as ucal.edu or leeds.ac.uk) to maintain a kind of virtual intranet. Business users became interested in this, and when Facebook reached out beyond the academic world (while still maintaining a robust presence within it), it found a ready market with large scale businesses - for example, the BBC has a network. Publications can be promoted through these networks: and this is just the start. Once someone has built their network of contacts, they can access the friends of friends, so the linking process is viral in nature; and they can also build groups and create events. This can be a powerful tool for book promotion, and as a no-cost relationship marketing tool it can be excellent. Publishers and individual authors organise book launches through it, and some use it to create fan clubs and reading groups, or support groups between authors. Students use it widely to keep in touch with academics and authors, developing a dialogue about specific publications and research topics. The downside is that Facebook is largely a closed network: as it is not possible to browse people's profiles, it is also not possible to discover subscribers whom the user does not know very easily. Technically, it's extremely robust and well designed, though profiles can not be personalised visually. A plus for some users (and a minus for others) is that Facebook has now allowed third-party developers to create extra applications, and they have added a dizzying range of tools, most of them fun and purely for recreational use.

1.17.2 MySpace[89]

MySpace is a similar tool to Facebook, but open in nature. It allows people to create a branded profile which is unique and reflects the personality of the owner in some way. It's clunky, folksy, quite frustrating to use at first, and has a feel of containing a wilder and more amateur community. It has been said that Facebook is for 'grads and execs' and MySpace is for 'the rest of us'. It is used extensively by musicians, and is an effective tool for building fan clubs and raising awareness. It can be freely browsed from the Web and is very much a public site. Many people also make use

89 www.myspace.com

of MySpace blogs. The blogging tools are unsophisticated, but the accessible quirky nature of MySpace has resulted in an impressive range of profiles and blogs: part of the fun can be running multiple profiles and linking them in creative ways. Harper Perennial have become masters at using this to market books: every book seems to have a profile, and they are adept at building networks of 'friends'. 'Friending' and 'defriending' is part of the language of MySpace, and being added as a friend often involves thanking someone for 'the add' by posting comments on their profile. This facility of commenting on people's profiles adds another context to social networking sites, as users can vote for and against people and their work. For books it therefore acts as a sort of reviewing tool – and like all reviews, can create an unsettling as well as a positive experience for those on the receiving end. MySpace users typically spend 20 minutes a day on their profiles - an astonishingly high average of web-committed time. MySpace feels more democratic and 'alternative' than Facebook.

1.17.3 Second Life[90]

Second Life is more akin to a vast downloadable interactive game, not dissimilar to the online gaming communities that children use every day (e.g., RuneQuest). Unlike Facebook and MySpace, it is not a Web-enabled tool, but a downloadable client linked to a huge interactive space. This space has become a 'sexy' and trendy place to do business, trade and occupy territory. In similar fashion to MySpace and Facebook, the user creates a profile, though of a new virtual entity - a new person (or 'avatar'), rather than a profile about themselves. They can use this virtual second life to explore a wide range of social interactions. Second Life is very free-flowing and creative, but it makes big demands on the user's time. He or she has to learn how to create and modify their appearance, build architectural structures and occupy land, and travel. For authors, it is a land without limits, and since the introduction of virtual cash, has become a place where they and their publishers can sell their books and book-related events.

90 http://secondlife.com/

1.17.4 Bebo[91]

Bebo is the home-grown British version of MySpace, with the difference that its demographic is very young – so it is a good destination for authors who write books for teenagers, cult fiction, etc. and for some secondary education titles. Individuals and companies marketing all sorts of goods and services to pre-teens and teenagers use it quite extensively. (Children can, of course, be unforgiving, and a lot of the social interactions revolve around 'dissing' people and products – so by joining it people are taking a calculated risk.)

1.17.5 Flickr[92]

Flickr is an image and video hosting website, web services suite and online community platform. In addition to being a popular website for users to share personal photographs, the service is widely used by bloggers as a photo repository. In October 2009 it claimed to host more than 4 billion images. Flickr asks photo submitters to organise images using tags which allow searchers to find images related to particular topics, such as place-names or subject-matter. Flickr was also one of the early websites to implement tag 'clouds', which provide access to images tagged with the most popular keywords.

Flickr also allows users to organise their photos into "sets", or groups of photos that fall under the same heading. It is particularly good for promoting illustrated books, or for sharing information about author events, or anything related to publishing for which photographs can act as effective promotional tools.

1.17.6 Twitter[93]

Twitter is a free social networking and microblogging service that enables its users to send and read messages known as tweets. Tweets are text-based posts of up to 140 characters displayed on the author's profile page and delivered to the author's subscribers, who are known as followers.

---

91   www.bebo.com
92   www.flickr.com
93   http://twitter.com

Senders can restrict delivery to those in their circle of friends or, by default, allow open access. Users can send and receive tweets via the Twitter website, Short Message Service (SMS) or external applications. While the service costs nothing to use, accessing it through SMS may incur phone service provider fees.

Twitter has grown hugely in popularity over the past year, precipitated by use of it to record impressions on events of national or international interest as they happen. It is quick and easy to use, unlike some of the other social networks, which require significant dedication in terms of time and expertise.

Publishers have used it for the following:

- Market intelligence: tweeters can send each other potentially interesting links to check out without wasting a lot of words on explanation (the latter is impossible, as the number of words that can be used in any one message is very restricted).

- Sharing views on happenings at trade events, such as book launches, conferences, book fairs and exhibitions, as they happen if you are attending (or 'eavesdropping' on them if you are not).

- Customer engagement. A quicker, more efficient way of getting customer feedback than inviting customers to contribute to a blog.

1.17.7 Delicious[94]

Delicious is a social bookmarking web service for storing, sharing and discovering web bookmarks. Use of it is free. It uses a non-hierarchical classification system in which users can tag each of their bookmarks with freely-chosen index terms. All bookmarks posted are publicly viewable by default, although users can mark specific bookmarks as private, and imported bookmarks are private by default. The public aspect of the site

94 http://delicious.com/

is emphasised. Its potential role for publishers in the promotion of new titles or authors is obvious.

1.17.8 Social networks in non-Anglophone countries

It is important for publishers seeking to use social netware to address new markets that the ones most common to the English-speaking world may be almost unheard of elsewhere. Recent research[95] has shown that Facebook is the most dominant social media force in North America and Europe, and now has 200 million plus users. However the largest social media forum of all is QQ[96], the most popular instant messaging network in China, which currently has more than 300 million users. In South America, Facebook is generally the most popular application, except in Brazil, where it is Orkut[97], a social networking and discussion site operated by Google. India also prefers Orkut. Other favourite social networks are very country-specific: for example, Hi5[98] in Mexico, Nasza-klasa[99] in Poland, Maktoob[100] in Libya, Cyworld[101] in South Korea, Lidé[102] in the Czech Republic, Iwiw[103] in Hungary and Odnoklassniki[104] in Moldavia. Interestingly, many of these sites can also be accessed in English.

The opportunities offered by social netware have mainly been described here within the context of how individual authors and small publishers have been using them, though some large publishing houses have certainly taken advantage of them as well, and if they are academic publishers, sometimes in collaboration with academics at the more forward-thinking universities. Mainstream publishers will undoubtedly exploit them much more in the future, as widgets become more and more common. Amazon has already exploited widget technology extensively. Widgets grew out of the e-book industry, but have the wider application of helping to promote books in all formats.

95 The research was carried out by Vincenzo Consenza, Director of Digital PR. See
    www.readwriteweb.com/archives/post_2.php
96 www.qq.com
97 www.orkut.com/About.aspx
98 http://hi5.com
99 http://nasza-klasa.pl
100 http://en.maktoob.com
101 http://us.cyworld.com
102 www.lide.cz
103 http://iwiw.hu/pages/user/login.jsp
104 www.odnoklassniki.ru

1.18   Aggregators

Some publishers, however, will prefer to sell their e-books through aggregators; and most publishers who have their own electronic platforms sell through several aggregators as well, on the same principle that they would place their print books with several different booksellers. Publishers with large e-book collections on their own platforms may choose to is that they can select publications from many different publishers on the same platform.

The main e-book aggregators are listed below.

1.18.1 Books24x7[105]

Books24x7 is an American company that offers an aggregated collection specialising in I.T. and Business books. Customers are divided between corporate and academic, so the platform is particularly useful for publishers trying to reach corporate prospects who can otherwise be hard to identify. Although the lion's share of its income derives from the US, Books24x7 has clients in many countries.

Publishers providing content for the subscription model have to accept Books24x7's charging methods, which are non-negotiable. For corporate subscriptions, an annual fee provides named users with unlimited access to the collections for which they are subscribing, including new content added during the subscription period.   There is no maintenance fee.

The publisher's suggested list price for the book is used to calculate royalties. The publisher is not required to set a price for the online edition. Books24x7 believes that it is fairest to use a publicly quoted suggested price for the print edition. Publisher royalties are paid in proportion to the amount of the usage that an individual book attracts, not to the proportion of the content supplied by the publisher. Publishers receive royalty cheques quarterly from Books24x7, based on an algorithmic formula of the content accessed by all of its users. Royalties are paid quarterly, by cheque. Books24x7 can create collections ranging from a handful of books to several thousand. Downloading of content at the chapter

---

105 http://library.books24x7.com/

level is managed by Books24x7 through the Chapters to Go program, but governed by the terms of the publisher agreement. Technically, the downloading facility can be switched on or off for all titles in a given imprint. It is only switched on if previous permission has been granted by the owners of the book content.

The 'Libraries' available consist of the following collections:

- ITPro
- BusinessPro
- FinancePro
- EngineeringPro
- ExecBlueprints
- ExecSummaries
- GovEssentials
- OfficeEssentials
- HospitalityPro
- Well-BeingEssentials
- AnalystPerspectives

Plus three non-English collections in French, German, and Spanish.

Customised 'bundles' can also be created for unique requirement 'at price points that are market driven'.

The following is an example of a bundle: The Project Management Institute (PMI) bundles a custom created 200 book "PMI specific" library with its membership fee. Books24x7 receives a fixed fee per year, and in return gives all PMI members access to the customised, privately-labelled site, which is maintained through Books24x7's integration/implementation services. Users enjoy single sign-on facilities, with member management and authentication handled by B24x7 via its implementation procedures.

Books24x7 produces a comprehensive range of printed and electronic marketing materials. It has a direct sales force whose key role is to open negotiations with corporate subscribers. Once it has closed a deal, it says that it conducts deeper, account-manager-driven activities to help promote usage within an organisation, using methods such as internal webinars, CTO emails, internal advertising and similar techniques.

Each week, it adds between 50 and 100 new titles to the databases and a 'New Book Alert' Email is sent to each subscriber, informing them of the new titles that have been added to their collection. These alerts are user-configurable and may be managed to suit the needs of subscribers. The level of effort expended is commensurate with the size of the account – some clients buy access to the product for many thousands of employees, and are supported accordingly. As a result of this activity, Books24x7 says that its renewal rate is more than 90 per cent.

Books24x7 holds local CAFÉ events and a Perspectives Conference that is attended by more than 500 people. It regularly attends publisher events such as BookExpo, the London Book Fair, and Frankfurt Book Fair.

Under the existing model, sales are computed via a publisher royalty pool, with a percentage paid on usage to publishers for each title. Different business models could be set in place for a large aggregated collection: for example, micro-payments for each page view, fee for full PDF download, aggregated library bundles, etc. There is also in operation a 'publisher reporting site', which offers statistics on content usage to select publishers only (method of selection of these publishers not given); this feature could be enhanced to include other reports if required.

1.18.2 Dawsonera[106]

Dawsonera is an ebook platform specifically designed to meet the expectations of academic libraries. It integrates with the existing Dawson library supply services that have been used by libraries for many years. Librarians can research e-book titles in the same web-catalogue that they use to locate printed books. The processing of EDI orders, account management, new title alerting, and the electronic delivery of catalogue records for both print and e-books are all performed by one single back-office software engine.

The Dawsonera model offers librarians the opportunity to purchase ebooks individually for perpetual ownership. It is not a subscription model. It has safeguards and limits in place to ensure that libraries buy multiple copies for heavily used titles, just as they do when buying printed books.

---

106 www.dawsonera.com

Any publisher whose books have appeal to libraries in universities, colleges, research institutes, government departments or corporate information departments is welcome to provide titles for sale via Dawsonera. What Dawson requires in order to host the e-books are 'web-ready' PDFs. This means that at the typesetting stage publishers should ask not only for a printer's PDF (for book production) but also a web-ready PDF. In the early stages of production, these can be produced for little or no extra cost by whomever has been contracted to provide the print-ready files. Retrospective conversion will incur some costs. No other formats are currently supplied by Dawson.

The PDF version of the title should have its own unique ISBN assigned to it by the publisher (sometimes referred to as an 'eISBN'). If the PDF is to be supplied to other aggregators in addition to Dawson, Dawson recommends that the publisher still only assigns one ISBN. (Rationale: it is not necessary to assign multiple ISBNs by supplier, but separate ISBNs are needed for each format. As Dawson only uses PDFs, each e-book will therefore have only one ISBN.)

Additionally, Dawson would like to receive metadata relating to the titles in an Excel spreadsheet. The minimum metadata elements required are:

- ISBN (10 or 13)
- eISBN (ie: an ISBN for the PDF format)
- Title
- Author/Editor
- Publication Date
- Edition (only req'd if not 1st)
- Imprint (if different to publisher name)
- File name
- Cover image file name (as Dawson likes to display thumbnails when it can)
- Price

If the publisher can supply JPEG images of the front cover (not the whole jacket) these will be added to Dawsonera to make the title record look more interesting. These images are of the type that the publisher may already be using on its own website and a low resolution is all that is required. Delivery of content and associated data is preferred via FTP.

Dawson can set up an FTP site to allow content to be sent to it, or can take content from the publisher's own FTP site. An alternative is for content and associated data to be delivered on CD-ROM.

A formal licence agreement needs to be signed. A standard template (boiler-plate) contract is available for consideration (unless the publisher prefers to use its own form of licence). The financial terms between Dawson and the publishers will be negotiated as part of the discussions prior to signature. Payment for sales will be made on a monthly basis in any currency the publisher chooses and by cheque or bank transfer with accompanying sales report and remittance advice.

Dawsonera allows online and offline reading of e-books but prevents all copying or cloning of titles. There are very strict DRM protocols in place to block any attempt at piracy. The Dawsonera software will permit a reader to copy or print only a very small proportion of the e-book they are reading. The amount set is deemed to be within the guidelines of 'fair dealing' or 'fair use' under copyright law. This can never be exceeded by the reader, even when reading the same e-book at a later date.

Dawsonera has more than 100,000 e-book titles available for purchase. Its focus is on recent titles with a strong academic appeal. Dawsonera's current market is HE institutions in the UK and Northern Europe. Its prior reach as a library supplier has allowed it to introduce the Dawsonera platform rapidly into many export markets for which e-books have a growing appeal.

1.18.3 Ebooks.com/EBL[107]

Ebook Corporation is an Australian company which has achieved worldwide popularity because of its innovative and flexible pricing models (some of which have now been emulated by other aggregators). It is especially strong in the US, Australia and the UK. It offers both retail and institutional 'solutions'.

---

107 http://publishers.ebookscorporation.com/

The publisher sets the e-book list price. In practice, this has meant:

- E-books sold to consumers are priced at a discount to the cheapest hardcopy edition – usually 20 per cent. (So, if the paperback is $19.95, the e-book version is $15.95)

- E-books sold to libraries are usually priced at the hardcopy list price. Some publishers choose the hardcover price, others the paperback.

- As a foreign supplier, EBC does not levy local sales taxes (such as VAT). Publishers are paid an agreed royalty.

Retail customers do not pay set-up or maintenance fees – just the price of the e-book. Institutional customers pay a platform fee on top of e-book list price. The platform fee and annual maintenance fee can either be paid upfront as a one-off fee, or incrementally as e-books are purchased. The annual maintenance fee is due one year after the platform fee is paid (either up-front or incrementally), and is discounted by 25 per cent if paid up-front; if the library prefers, it can be paid incrementally. This is not shared with the publisher.

Publishers are paid quarterly by US dollar cheque. Payments are accompanied by a detailed sales report.

EBC has standard (global) rules that apply to all of its titles. Permissions are declared up-front to the end-user, and are managed and enforced by server-side and client-side technology. These are as follows:

Retail

- **Printing:** The user may print one complete copy of the book every year. This is managed through the online reader to prevent abuse. Pages can only be printed one at a time which significantly limits possibilities of abuse. The user might also print limited amounts (if the publisher has chosen to allow this) if the e-book is downloaded to their PC.

- **Copy-Paste:** Up to, but no more than, 10 per cent of the book may be copied to the user's clipboard in any 30 day period. Pages can only be copied one at a time which significantly limits possibilities of abuse. The user might also copy limited amounts (if the publisher has chosen to allow this) if the e-book is downloaded to their PC.

Institutional

Patrons are allowed 20 per cent printing and 5 per cent copying per book per patron.

Pricing models:

- **Book-by-Book Retail Sales:** A consumer pays by credit card for perpetual online access to the work (via the online reader) and the ability to download the book to their computer and/or handheld device.

- **Book-by-Book Institutional Sales:** A library pays for perpetual online access to the work (via the online reader) and the ability to download the book to patrons' computers.

- **Bundles:** EBL now releases starter subject bundles, comprised of 100 best-selling titles in select subjects offered at a discounted price.

1.18.4   Ebrary[108]

Ebrary has a particularly strong client base in the USA, the UK and the Scandinavian countries. It has two main pricing models, the perpetual access model and the subscription model. The publisher sets the price for Ebrary's perpetual access sales model. Ebrary uses a pricing algorithm for the subscription model which takes into consideration a number of factors, including library FTE and title usage. Publisher remuneration is based on this. For the perpetual access model, publisher remuneration

---

108 www.ebrary.com/corp

is based on an agreed split of the cover price of the book between Ebrary and the publisher.

Subscription pricing combines the cost of the content and technology licences. For customers that purchase titles, fees for platform hosting are assessed separately from the cost of content. This income is not shared with the publishers. Organisations that wish to obtain a licence to host their own digital content on the Ebrary platform are charged separately for hosting and submission. In this way, the platform may be used as a type of institutional repository. Hosting fees are also not shared with publishers.

1.18.5 Knovel[109]

Knovel is a sophisticated aggregated platform which focuses on e-books on the 'hard' sciences, engineering and I.T. It offers a range of interactive applications, including drop-down boxes which allow users to perform and check their own scientific and mathematical calculations. More than fifty publishers supply it with specialised content. Its customers include 75 of the Fortune 500 companies and over 300 leading engineering and science universities worldwide. It uses a number of resellers in order to address different sectors and markets[110].

Knovel determines how much content can be downloaded and printed out by patrons, although publishers can have an influence on this. Knovel also determines the final prices charged, and whether the books are sold individually or as a whole collection, though the starting-point is usually the list-price of the publisher's hardback title. Prices listed and sent to customers include VAT.

Pricing models used include annual subscription, for collections and bundles supplied to libraries, and outright sale for individual titles supplied to end-users. Libraries pay an annual maintenance fee. Publishers are paid royalties on a percentage of sales basis. If payment is for part of a licenced collection, Knovel calculates the correct amount by means of a formula which takes into consideration the publisher's list price for the

109 http://why.knovel.com/
110 http://why.knovel.com/partners/resellers.html

content, its age, number of pages supplied, interactivity added, etc. Publishers are paid on a quarterly basis, sixty days after the close of the quarter. Publishers in the disciplines relevant to Knovel report that they derive a significant income stream from working with Knovel.

1.18.6 MyiLibrary (Ingram Digital)[111]

MyiLibrary is now able to offer what is arguably the largest aggregated e-book collection. It is strong in the UK, Canada and the USA. Some of the big American and Canadian research universities use the MyiLibrary platform exclusively for e-books. It also operates in other countries, notably in Europe.

The price of the book is set by the publisher. VAT and applicable taxes are not included in the price of the book. This is added separately to assist users who reclaim VAT. Bundles and / or collections from one or more publishers are driven by customer needs and requirements. Therefore, titles are chosen by the customer, MyiLibrary distributors and Ingram Digital working together. Individual publishers can also put collections of their own works together and offer them on the platform. The aggregator is flexible about the amount and nature of content included. Ongoing sales reports are provided that show what has been sold, and publishers are welcome to audit these figures if they wish.

MyiLibrary users can choose from the following options:

- Single and multi-concurrent user book pricing, which means that libraries (and individuals) can buy on a book-by-book basis, allowing single use or multiple users to access the book(s) bought.

- Single and multi-concurrent user pricing for set collections.

- Individual publisher bundle arrangements where back content may be priced as a bundle or a set publisher collection may be priced as a bundle.

---

111 www.myilibrary.com

- Annual subscription options for bundles and collections.

Publishers are remunerated on a quarterly basis for all sales. There is a clear audit trail for all content sold, to which publishers are made party. There is no shared revenue pool; each publisher receives what is owed for the sale of its books. Ingram Digital and the publisher agree the retail price that will be used for each pricing model. Ingram Digital negotiates a discount on that price: e.g., if the book is sold for $100 and the discount is 60 per cent, the publisher receives $40. This system is common to all the sales models. There is a modest per-institution annual maintenance fee which is not shared with the publisher.

With regard to printing/download permissions, the Ingram Digital team will work with each publisher to establish individual requirements. The system allows for book-by-book variation if the publisher requires, but says that it is confusing for users. Therefore, Ingram Digital tries to get common agreement from all publishers as to what is generally allowable, and has so far succeeded in achieving this.

Ingram Digital has set up MyiLibrary librarian user groups both in the UK and North America. These groups meet half-yearly and provide guidance and feedback with regards to all aspects of the product including functionality, content and customer services.

1.18.7 NetLibrary[112]

NetLibrary is the oldest of the e-book aggregators, and probably still has more customers worldwide than any of the others. Its customer base includes both public and academic libraries, and it is strong in both sectors.

When working with NetLibrary, the publisher establishes the price at which titles will be sold. When opportunities are identified for special offers or sales programmes, prices are set by mutual negotiation.

NetLibrary's standard pricing model resembles the traditional print sales model. The library selects titles individually (observing the minimum sales

---

112 www.netlibrary.com

requirement of 100 copies when its collection is started) and pays the retail hard cover price that has been set by the publisher. In addition, it pays an access (or maintenance) fee, which can be paid either as a one-off charge of 55 per cent of the retail price, or 15 per cent of the retail price annually for as many years as they wish access to be available to their patrons. The maintenance fee is not shared with the publishers. NetLibrary is experimenting with other types of pricing model as well.

NetLibrary usually negotiates a discount with publishers which is then recorded in the contract. Publishers are paid according to the agreed discount on a monthly basis, with payment being received 45 days after the close of the payment month, for each title sold. If a unique pricing or payment programme is developed with an individual publisher, payment terms are captured in a similar way for the former, or as an exceptional agreement for the latter.

1.18.8 Numilog[113]

Numilog is probably the most important e-book aggregator not working primarily in the English language. There are many English-language books within its collection, and British and American publishers report good sales from the titles that they have placed with the company. It was founded in 2000, and in 2008 became a subsidiary of Hachette Livre. All of the e-book titles that it holds are DRM protected, and it also offers audiobooks. The platform carries more than 100,000 e-book titles and a substantial collection of audiobooks. Numilog also supplies the platform for e-books for the visually disadvantaged in France[114].

The business model is pay-per-view for individual users or via a licence based on the number of readers and the duration of lending for libraries. The latter includes 'electronic lending' of books for an agreed period of time. Either using their ID or terminals in the library, students and academics can download e-books to their PCs or their PDAs as time-limited loans. Numilog posts its standard contract for publishers on its website.

---

113 www.numilog.net/accueil.asp
114 http://bnh.numilog.com

1.18.9 Safari Books Online[115]

The Safari platform is aimed primarily at the corporate sector, but is also widely bought by HEIs. It is strongest in the US, but also has customers in many other countries. The 9,000 electronic learning and reference resources currently on the platform – predominantly in Computing and Business - come from such leading publishers as O'Reilly Media, Addison-Wesley, Peachpit Press, Apress, Manning and Talented Pixie. Publishers new to Safari are invited to make contact. The platform contains training videos, rough cuts, short cuts and articles. Collections and bundles are sold or licensed to institutional customers. Whole book and chapter downloads can be delivered to end users' PCs or mobile devices.

The subscription service bears no relation to publishers' list prices, but the outright sales model is based on them. For the licensed model, calculations are based on the proportion of the publishers' content used over the period. Royalties are paid on a quarterly basis.

1.19   E-books for the reading impaired

Many countries, particularly the UK, the USA and Canada, have recognised that digital delivery – via e-books, audio or Print on Demand in Large Print format – can offer solutions for the reading impaired. The most common of these is sight impairment, but the term can also be used to include people with learning disabilities or any cognitive or physical disability that makes it difficult or impossible for someone to read the standard edition of a book. E-books can offer advantages to reading impaired readers, including the facility to change the size or font of the typeface or the automatic conversion of the book to a 'talking book' via speech synthesising software.

Most publishers want to support initiatives for the reading impaired for philanthropic reasons. However, there are also sound commercial reasons for engaging in this type of publishing: a) it offers the potential for a new revenue stream and b) legislation that has now been passed in several countries means that the publisher has an obligation to offer source files to reading impaired readers upon demand. If the publisher

---

115 www.safaribooksonline.com

has not made a book requested by an individual commercially available in a suitable format, it can be converted to one by organisations such as the RNIB on a one-off, non-commercial basis. This modus operandi is immensely costly to the organisation footing the bill, and does not benefit the publisher or author by helping them to reach the full potential market for the title in the new format which results.

More publishers are therefore considering pre-empting the one-off requests by addressing the market themselves. However, the challenges to publishers are considerable, even if they are prepared to digitise not only new frontlist but also backlist titles - and many publishers do not have the resource, or in some cases the rights, to do the latter.

The Digital Accessible Information System[116] (DAISY) Consortium was formed in 1996 with the aim of further developing accessibility standards for people who are reading impaired. Publishers interested in making their publications commercially available to reading impaired readers will find a great deal of advice and technical specifications on the DAISY website. It is worth noting that if publishers place DRM protections on e-books, this can prevent text-to-speech applications from converting the text to synthesised voice output. On the plus side, ePub is based on the same underlying standard on which the standard DAISY format has been built[117].

1.20   Audio books

The audiobook market has grown quickly in the Anglophone countries over the past decade. The latest survey by the American Audio Publishers Association[118] (APA), carried out in 2008, found that the total value of the audiobook market was then approximately US$1bn, a 12 per cent increase from when the survey was previously carried out in 2006. The Canadian market has grown by 8 –10 per cent in this period. The USA leads the market. 28 per cent of all American adults listened to an audiobook in 2008 (the figure was 25 per cent in 2006). CD sales represented 72 per cent of the market, and audio downloads 21 per cent of the market.

---

116 www.daisy.org
117 This is the DTBook standard from NISO.
118 see www.audiopub.org/resources-industry-data.asp

Sales of pre-loaded devices had increased significantly since 2006, and made up 3 per cent of the market. Cassette sales remained static at 3 per cent of the market. There was a continuing marked trend for consumers to prefer unabridged books to the abridged versions which were popular when the audiobook market was first developed. In 2006 unabridged books accounted for 68 per cent of the US market: In 2008 the figure was 85 per cent. This trend is mirrored in the UK, where in 2006 (the last year for which the recently disbanded Audio Publishers Association[119] published figures) unabridged books accounted for 60 per cent of sales and abridged books for 40 per cent.

The audiobook market was consumer-led until recently, but now libraries – public libraries in particular – account for many of the sales. The APA website lists details both of publishers active in the audiobook market and of third parties willing to sell audiobooks on their behalf. Some of the big e-book aggregators – e.g., NetLibrary, MyiLibrary - now sell audiobooks as part of their offer to libraries. Audible[120] and Amazon are the biggest retailers of audiobooks in both North America and the UK (Audible was taken over by Amazon in 2008 and now operates as a subsidiary company). As well as the US, Canada and the UK, Audible also has significant numbers of customers in Australia, France, Germany, India, Ireland, Pakistan, Russia and Spain.

From the publisher's point of view, audiobooks offer exciting growth opportunities at a time when print book sales are more or less static. However, the costs are not insignificant. E-books are relatively cheap to produce, but the creation of an audiobook requires a significant outlay, largely caused by the need to record a master file. A commercial audiobook typically incurs $10,000 plus recording costs (although partnering arrangements between publishers and recording studios can reduce this cost by up to one half).

Electronic rights are required in order to produce audiobooks, just as they are required for e-books (sometimes 'electronic rights' will embrace both, sometimes audio rights have to be specified or negotiated separately). Global rights are probably less of an issue for audio books, because

119 www.theapa.net/figures20052006.php
120 www.audible.co.uk; www.audible.com

often national editions are required, even for countries where people speak the same language used in the original work, resulting in dual US and UK editions, for example. Following years of controversy about Napster, piracy is perhaps even more of a worry than for e-books for audiobook publishers and retailers. DRM is therefore frequently applied; but publishers should be aware of the fact that, from the retailer's point of view, proprietary DRM also has the effect of locking them in to the retailer's sales channel. For example, prior to Audible's takeover by Amazon, it operated an exclusive distribution arrangement with Apple's iTunes store, and sold audiobooks on iTunes on condition that the files incorporated Apple's 'Fairplay' DRM system. Amazon scrapped this deal after the acquisition took place; and generally publishers are becoming much more flexible about DRM arrangements, despite the inherent risks, because they are unpopular with consumers. Random House, Penguin and Simon and Schuster have all relaxed the DRM arrangements that they put in place when first entering the market.

1.20.1 Pricing audiobooks

Audiobooks supplied on cassette or CD are generally higher priced than a comparable hardcover print edition. This reflects the additional cost of production. Pre-loaded digital formats are priced much more competitively, but at present only account for a small part of the market. Downloadable audiobooks are generally priced at a point between the print hardback and paperback editions, and there is evidence that this price could drop further. In 2006, Bowker carried out a study which reported that the average list price for unabridged audio titles was US$41.26, compared with the average list price for adult hardbacks of US$27.55. Some of the large retailers – for example, Audible and Canada's Simply Audiobooks[121] - offer subscription pricing models as well as discrete list prices, which reflects the requirements of the large and growing library market for which they also cater.

---

121 www.simplyaudiobooks.com

1.21   Digital Printing: "Print on Demand" (POD)

Digital printing has been so well-publicised during the past decade that there can now be few publishers who are not familiar with the concept[122]. Sometimes described as the "quiet revolution" of the book industry, it is now adopted by many publishers to enable them to reissue out-of-print backlist titles economically in order to fulfil a definite continuing demand that does not, however, warrant a full offset-litho reprint. Led by Lightning Source, right from the start Print on Demand companies have sought to persuade publishers that the solutions that they offer should inform the publisher's development of its strategy, rather than being regarded merely as an additional production tool. This concept has been aided both by rapid technological advances in digital printing, and by the rise of DAMs and DADs. Leading publishers now see the production of print books, e-books, audio books, and Print on Demand books as part of a continuous process in which the content is commissioned, developed, reviewed and managed by the publisher and the format chosen by the customer.

Originally the preserve mainly of academic publishers or self-publishing companies, digital printing is now being adopted by trade publishers, and publishers from all sectors are experimenting with using it for frontlist titles as well as backlist. There are still some constraints: digital printing may not be economically viable for certain types of publication, such as trade paperbacks; colour digital printing is expensive; and the quality of half-tone illustrations may not match those of offset-litho printed books (though the latest generation of digital printers has almost achieved this). In addition, not all digital printing companies offer all of the trim sizes that publishers would like. Although digital printing works from specially-converted PDFs, the most economical way for publishers to exploit it is to put all their content into XML format right from the start. POD PDFs cannot be used in the exact format in which they have been prepared in order to produce e-books, but the conversion process from the print PDF to e-book format is easier and cheaper than from print copy to e-book format. Some conversion companies offer a dual POD/e-book conversion process.

---

122   For those who are not familiar with digital printing, or who would like a quick refresher, Section 3.4 offers a brief account of how it works.

1.21.1 Print on Demand: retail

Digital printing companies dislike the term "Print on Demand" and try to persuade publishers and bibliographic agencies to make no distinction between digitally-printed books and those produced by offset litho, as this can have the effect of dissuading booksellers from stocking these titles (largely owing to folk-memories of badly-produced self-published books in the past, and more recent difficulties with discounts and returns procedures which have now for the most part been resolved). This campaign has been successful, and some publishers (especially those using POD for 'ultra-short print runs') now supply bookshops with titles printed by either method without mentioning the fact. However, an exciting innovation in digital printing is the advent of machinery which can actually produce titles truly 'on demand' in a retail setting.

1.21.2 Printing in the shop

A company called On Demand Books[123] has marketed the Espresso Book Machine, a relatively compact product which can print, bind and trim on demand at point of sale perfect-bound paperback books with four-colour covers in minutes, rather than hours. As sophisticated as the machine itself is the accompanying administration software, which ensures that publishers' content is secure and automatically tracks all jobs and remits royalty payments. The print standard is described by On Demand Books as of 'library quality', and whilst the finished product is neither indistinguishable from offset litho nor of the same high standard as Print on Demand books produced on larger machines in factory conditions, the quality is certainly acceptable, particularly if this method is the only way that the end-user can secure the book other than by trawling second-hand bookshops and websites.

123 See www.ondemandbooks.com/home.htm

1.22 Virtual Learning Environments (VLEs) and e-learning support systems

1.22.1 A note on terminology

A number of terms are in use to describe e-learning support systems; some of these are interchangeable and others refer to specific types of system. Further difficulty is caused by the use of different terms to mean the same thing (or slightly different things!) in different geographical regions. The following short note may help to dispel some of the confusion.

A VLE is a computer programme which enables educational or training products and information to be disseminated digitally. It may therefore be used to facilitate a full e-learning programme, or merely act as an aid to the distribution of reading lists, lecture notes, etc. A system which supports e-learning is sometimes also called a Learning Management System (LMS), a Content Management System (CMS), a Learning Content Management System (LCMS), a Managed Learning Environment (MLE), a Learning Support System (LSS), an Online Learning Centre (OLC) or a Learning Platform (LP). CMS and LMS are the terms most commonly used in the US; but it should be noted that the latter one is usually applied to software for the management of corporate training programmes, rather than for mainstream educational purposes.

In the UK and most of Europe, the term VLE is used most frequently, if sometimes incorrectly. Strictly speaking, a VLE is a less comprehensive application than an MLE. The latter can refer to the wider infrastructure of information systems within the organisation that support electronic learning, and in some cases could even include the physical environment within which learning is delivered. In the UK, the recently-disbanded BECTA[124] used the term Learning Platform (LP) to indicate either an MLE or a VLE used within the schools sector. Learning platforms are becoming increasingly popular in schools in all of the Anglophone countries, and the market for publications and other products to support them is probably growing more rapidly than in other educational sectors. BECTA advised

---

124 www.becta.org.uk

that "..*at the heart of any learning platform is the concept of a personalised online learning space for the pupil. This space should offer teachers and pupils access to stored work, e-learning resources, communication and collaboration with peers, and the facility to track progress.*"

For publishers, providing profit-generating material for VLEs is not without its difficulties. If an Open Source application, such as the immensely popular Moodle, is being used, the application developer has no means of policing the way in which the publisher's material is used. Publishers wishing to make content available for VLEs therefore need to make very sure that it is securely protected if they wish to prevent file-sharing or unauthorised downloads. In higher education in particular, it is also often quite difficult to find out who is in charge of the VLE at a particular institution. It may be a librarian, an academic, or a technical support person. However, as the use of VLEs becomes more sophisticated, many institutions are appointing dedicated e-Learning Managers.

1.22.2 Blackboard[125]

Blackboard is the most prominent of the commercially-available VLEs. It develops and licenses VLE software applications and related services to more than 5,000 organisations in approximately 60 countries. Blackboard acquired WebCT, its closest rival, about four years ago. Its services are aimed at education at all levels, including HE and FE, businesses and government, and it has clients in all of these sectors. Products include:

- The Blackboard Academic Suite, consisting of

  - The Blackboard Learning System, a course management system
  - The Blackboard Community System, a community and portal system
  - The Blackboard Content System, a content and management system.

---

125 www.blackboard.com

- The Blackboard Commerce Suite, consisting of

  - The Blackboard Transaction System, a transaction processing system tied to university ID systems
  - The Blackboard Community System, an e-commerce front end for the transaction System
  - Bb One, a network of commercial and retail businesses that accept Blackboard-powered debit card transaction.

- The products originally developed by WebCT before it was taken over by Blackboard. These include:

  - Blackboard Vista, a course management system
  - Blackboard Campus Edition, a different kind of course management system.

Although Blackboard software is closed source (and therefore protects publishers' content), the company has developed open architecture (called Building Blocks) that can be used by patrons to extend the functionality of Blackboard products. Blackboard is licensed to clients. Royalties are paid to publishers for materials uploaded to the applications.

1.22.3 Moodle[126]

Worldwide, Moodle is probably the most-used VLE of all. This may in part be because it is an Open Source Course Management system (in other words, 'free'), but also because it is extremely flexible and works for all types of educational and business e-learning environment. Moodle originated in Australia. Its developers describe it as follows:

'The focus of the Moodle project is always on giving educators the best tools to manage and promote learning, but there are many ways to use Moodle:

- Moodle has features that allow it to scale to very large deployments and hundreds of thousands of students, yet it can also be used for a primary school or an education hobbyist.

---

126 http://moodle.org/

- Many institutions use it as their platform to conduct fully online courses, while some use it simply to augment face-to-face courses (known as blended learning).

- Many users like to use the activity modules (such as Forums, Wikis, Databases and so on) to build richly collaborative communities of learning around their subject matter (in the social constructionist tradition), while others prefer to use Moodle as a way to deliver content to students (such as standard SCORM packages) and assess learning using assignments or quizzes.'

However, for 'flexibility', publishers – and institutions – should not read 'simplicity'. Getting the best out of Moodle is quite complex; a number of manuals have been written on how to use it, directed at publishers as well as educators and business developers. Publishers thinking of making their content available via Moodle would be well-advised to consult one of these[127]. There can be little doubt that investing some time and resource in Moodle is worthwhile: as the software is open source, official registration is voluntary. Nevertheless, there are currently (June 2010) 49,665 registered Moodle sites in 213 countries[128]. There is also a demonstration site within the Moodle website, with instructions in most of the languages of the registered users[129]; and, for publishers feeling particularly industrious, a list of most of the registered institutions which, with some further work, would yield contact names for their e-learning managers, all potential customers for content[130].

1.22.4 Fronter[131]

Fronter also describes itself as an 'Open Source' platform (though there are costs attached to using it) and is also aimed at educational institutions at all levels and in all countries, though it seems to be particularly strong in the schools sector and in Europe. Its promotional materials are translated

---

127 Among the best are the manuals that can be purchased either in hard copy or e-book format from www.howtomoodle.com.
128 See http://moodle.org/stats
129 http://demo.moodle.org
130 http://moodle.org/sites
131 http://com.fronter.info

into English, Danish, Dutch, Finnish, French, Norwegian Polish, Russian and Swedish. It does not disclose how many clients use it, but claims that there are 'millions of teachers and learners at thousands of institutions around the world'. It offers almost one hundred 'easy to use' learning applications which are regularly updated according to user needs.

1.22.5 Microsoft Class Server[132]

Microsoft Class Server 4.0 is aimed at schools. It is currently available only in the USA and Canada (though Microsoft also offers other types of educational resource that can be acquired throughout the world [133]). It is a web-based learning management platform that supports personalised instruction. It can be used to deliver exercises and assignments for students and has the facility also to involve parents. Teachers can create curriculum content, and manage lessons online and offline. It supports the collection and analysis of student performance data in real time. Teachers can review student achievement, and identify areas of improvement faster, improving the quality of support. Reporting data can be collated automatically. Class Server has to be paid for, and is licensed, usually via third-party resellers.

1.22.6 Microsoft Learning Gateway

Microsoft Learning Gateway involves the use of the 'Sharepoint Learning Kit', which enables educators to create curriculum plans and assignments out of existing documents devised via Microsoft Office and other applications. Like Class Server, it includes assessment activities. It is aimed at institutions working in both secondary and tertiary education, and, also like Class Server, licensed through third parties. Currently it is available via third-party partners based in the USA, the UK, Australia, Egypt, France, the Netherlands and Romania.

---

132 www.microsoft.com/emea/education/learninggateway/classserver.mspx
133 www.microsoft.com/education/pil/RR_home.aspx

1.22.7 Rameseys

Ramesys is a schools solution, and particularly strong in the UK. It has won a number of contracts in the UK government's Building Schools for the Future initiative. Ramesys licenses its software and related software to schools.

1.23 Organisations that help publishers with publishing digitally

1.23.1 Support from central government

BECTA, The British Education and Communications Technology Agency, was abolished by the incoming Coalition Administration on 23rd May 2010. At present it is not clear whether this quango will be replaced by an alternative body with a national remit. If this proves not to be the case, individual schools and local authorities will continue to make decisions about purchasing software and hardware, but they will no longer have access to a government-approved organisation to advise them and endorse products.

1.23.2 Copyright Licensing Agency collective digital licences

The Copyright Licensing Agency Limited (CLA)[134] licenses organisations to copy extracts from magazines, books, journals and digital publications on behalf of authors, publishers and visual creators in the UK. It manages secondary but not primary rights – i.e., rights for activities which it is impractical or uneconomic for the publishers to license directly. It is therefore known as a 'Reproductive Rights Organisation' (RRO). Worldwide, there are more than fifty national RROs; collectively they belong to the International Federation of Reproductive Rights Organisations (IFRRO). Some of these organisations have bi-lateral reciprocal agreements, meaning that they license copying of titles belonging to each other's national repertoires and ensure mutual reimbursement for materials used.

---

134 www.cla.co.uk

The CLA has recently negotiated digital copying licences for schools and higher education institutions (HEI) for which it is paid fees that are then distributed to publishers. The HE Collective Digital Licence permits HEIs to make multiple photocopies and scan extracts from printed books, journals and magazines and in addition allows the copying and re-use of digital material such as electronic or online publications. It operates on an opt-in basis and has some fairly stringent terms and conditions designed to protect publishers, which may be viewed on the CLA website. It also offers a Photocopying and Scanning (i.e. excluding digital) HE Licence. Publishers may opt out of this licence or choose to restrict or deny the copying of certain publications. There are also some US publishers that are specifically excluded from all CLA licences.

These licences provide publishers with a source of income from digitisation (whether or not they offer digital products themselves) that would otherwise be lost to them.

Part Two | Opportunities

2.1   International projects

This section begins with giving details of some international digital projects
that are of interest to publishers wishing

to promote content digitally. They are
relevant for two reasons: firstly, these
projects and the organisations that they
support are interested in commercial
as well as not-for-profit or 'free' digital
publications; therefore, publishers can
develop opportunities to sell to them.
Secondly, they are examples of the way in which the world is moving
digitally. Publishers should be aware of the ambitions and quest for new
business models that such projects represent; and might like to consider
ways in which they will need to adapt their own business models and
ways of offering content in order to preserve their profitability.

2.1.1   The role of governments in 'going digital'

The subject of governments and their role in the move to digital is so
vast and pivotal that it really requires a report to itself. Various individual
country government initiatives are referred to in the relevant sections
below, particularly where they have a direct impact on publishing and
publishers. The following general points may also be helpful:

The role of government in the move to national and international digitisation
is complex and often contradictory. The governments of all of the countries
described in this report support the transition from print to electronic and
the widespread use of the Internet to disseminate information (albeit with
greater or lesser degrees of sophistication and commitment); but not all
are either actively or by implication supporting the commercial publishing
industry. This is because governments have more than one role to play in
the move to digitisation and often more than one agenda. Sometimes the
agendas can be contradictory, and often they are in competition with or
even militate against activity within the commercial sector.

Key roles of a government are:

- **As a funder and encourager** of national and international online networks.

- **As a promoter and encourager** (sometimes also as an official maker of mandatory decisions) of using online facilities for educational (at all levels) and business purposes.

- **As a publisher in its own right,** whose online publications complement those of established publishers.

- **As a competitor to publishers,** whose aim (stated or otherwise) may be to replace publishers' commercial products with 'free' products.

- **As a policy-maker.**

- **As an investor and innovator,** particularly of new hardware and software products. For example, the United States Defense Department has been a developer and early adopter of many software products and platforms[135] .

- Finally, it should be emphasised that **governments work together with other governments,** and with a series of other national and international NGOs. These organisations talk to each other about service and content providers, and will often choose the same ones on what is virtually a 'word-of-mouth' basis[136] .

---

135 Mark Logic is one company that has built revenues and reputation on work carried out for the US Defense Department
136 Several software suppliers have told me this; and Lightning Source UK, having made a start with one or two government organisations and NGOs, now has about 50 customers or strong leads in this field.

2.1.2   Google[137]

Google has added a raft of programmes to its interface over the years, many of which serve as supplements to publishers' offerings and sometimes providing new opportunities for publishers. A number of key programmes are explained below.

Google Scholar is a search engine focusing on scholarly literature. The search function covers articles, theses, books, abstracts and courts opinions. It sources content from academic publishers, professional societies, online repositories, universities and other websites. Publishers are able to include their publications on Google Scholar, and librarians are also invited to work with the programme to provide access to their content. Google has been permitted to scan libraries' out of copyright works in a range of countries.

Google Books is more prevalent in the US, but it offers a scanning service to collate thousands of books as part of Google's search function. The book-search covers a multitude of themes, such as finance, business, computers, relationships, literary criticism, law, humour and travel. It also offers a 'My Library' service which records and organises a user's collection of books for which they have searched, and which can be shared with other users. Google Books has also set up a more commercial area for publishers, amongst others, called the Partner Programme. It allows publishers to place their books on the search engine, with only a limited number of scanned pages available to users, who then have to decide whether to buy the book.

As an extension to Google Books, it has been announced that **Google Editions** was expected be launched in July 2010. This is a digital bookstore set up to showcase its scanned books, plus those of other retailers and businesses. Google claims to have already signed more than 25,000 publishers worldwide to the project. Unlike other online bookstores, Google Editions will be hosted through the 'cloud', meaning that the book content is stored online and is therefore accessible in any bookstore,

---

137 Information on how to participate can be found at http://books.google.com/googlebooks/
     publishers.html

e-reading device, mobile or computer. This means that consumers are not tied to specific operating systems or vendors. Publishers are signing up to place their titles with Google Editions for the following reasons:

- **They will use the e-Pub format,** and therefore be accessible on almost all e-readers, tablets, smartphones and PCs except for the Amazon Kindle (which uses a proprietary format and does not support ePub).

- **For the consumer, the huge number of titles available from a single source** will be compelling. Discoverability is still the greatest barrier to e-book sales. If consumers know that they can find the title in Google Editions, they are almost certain to go straight to the site.

- Google has stated its willingness to support the **agency pricing model,** which allows publishers to choose their level of profitability.

2.1.3   The European Library and Europeana

For a number of years the European Commission has been working on projects to boost the digital economy. These have prepared the ground

for an online service that is designed to bring together Europe's cultural heritage in one (virtual) place.

The idea for Europeana came from a letter to the Presidency of Council and to the Commission on 28 April 2005. Six Heads of State and Government suggested the creation of a virtual European Library, aiming to make Europe's cultural and scientific resources accessible for all.

On 30 September 2005 the European Commission published the i2010[138] Communication on digital libraries, in which it announced its strategy to promote and support the creation of a European digital library, as a

---

138 http://ec.europa.eu/information_society/activities/digital_libraries/index_en.htm

strategic goal within the European Information Society i2010 Initiative[139], which aims to foster growth and jobs in the information society and media industries. The European Commission's goal for Europeana is to make European information resources easier to use in an online environment. It will build on Europe's rich heritage, combining multicultural and multilingual environments, and 'free' material and commercially produced material, using technological advances and new business models.

The Europeana prototype is the result of a two-year project that began in July 2007. Europeana.eu went live on 20 November 2008. It is a Thematic Network funded by the European Commission under the eContentplus programme[140], as part of the i2010 policy[141]. Originally known as the European digital library network – EDLnet – it is a partnership of 100 representatives of heritage and knowledge organisations and IT experts from throughout Europe. They contribute to the Work Packages that are solving the technical and usability issues.

The project is run by a core team based in the national library of the Netherlands, the Koninklijke Bibliotheek[142]. It builds on the project management and technical expertise developed by The European Library[143], which is a service of the Conference of European National Librarians[144].

Overseeing the project is the EDL Foundation[145], which includes key European cultural heritage associations from the four domains[146]. The Foundation's statutes commit members to:

- Provide access to Europe's cultural and scientific heritage though a cross-domain portal

- Co-operate in the delivery and sustainability of the joint portal

---

139 http://ec.europa.eu/information_society/eeurope/i2010/index_en.htm
140 http://ec.europa.eu/information_society/activities/econtentplus/index_en.htm
141 http://ec.europa.eu/information_society/activities/digital_libraries/index_en.htm
142 www.kb.nl
143 http://search.theeuropeanlibrary.org/portal/en/index.html
144 www.nlib.ee/cenl/about.php
145 http://version1.europeana.eu/web/guest/edl-foundation
146 These are museums, audio-visual collections, libraries and archives.

- Formulate initiatives to bring together existing digital content

- Support digitisation of Europe's cultural and scientific heritage.

2.1.4 ARROW[147]

ARROW stands for Accessible Registries of Rights Information and

Orphan Works. ARROW's aim is to establish a single framework to identify rights information, supporting the development of Europeana. The project launched in autumn 2008 and will last for two and a half years. Like the European Library and Europeana, it is funded under the European Commission's eContentplus programme. ARROW provides tools and information to support policy. Its remit does not include the setting of policy itself.

The origins of the project lie in high-level discussions that have taken place between all the relevant stakeholders within Europe, including libraries, publishers and collective rights organisations. Their explicitly-stated vision is to maximise access to digital content by the user without compromising the rights of authors or other rightsholders. Consequently, the participating libraries need to know the copyright status of works they are planning to digitise and make available publicly. ARROW seeks to address the problem of identifying 'orphan works' in particular. These are works that are impossible to digitise because their rights status is unclear. If a solution cannot be found to the orphan works issue, digitisation programmes are likely to be left with a 'black hole' in which many twentieth-century works are missing, because the author may still be alive or have beneficiaries to his or her estate still able to make decisions about whether to allow the works to be copied or made available, but this information cannot be traced.

The challenge ARROW aims to overcome is the fragmentation of the rights information infrastructure that exists at present. The project proposes to create a seamless service principally across a distributed

147 www.arrow-net.eu

network of national databases containing information about the rights status of works. This infrastructure, once established, will provide valuable tools for libraries and other organisations to contact rights holders in seeking copyright clearance for the use of content. The other key strand of the ARROW project is to increase the level of interoperability between public domain and commercial content, leading to innovative business models for the exposure and use of, and where appropriate payment for, digital content.

The project currently focuses on books, but could be extended to other types of material in the future: for example, journals, newspapers, images, archives, etc.

In the UK, ARROW is being co-ordinated by the British Library and the Copyright licensing Agency, and is supported by The Publishers Association, the Publishers Licensing Society, the Authors' Licensing and Collecting Society, WATCH and Nielsen BookData.

In the USA, OCLC has already embarked on a similar project. Prior to the inception of ARROW, it had already designed and begun to implement astrategy designed to harness the technology and capabilities of its US member libraries to create the first web-scale co-operative library management service. OCLC plans to release web-scale circulation, print and electronic acquisitions, and license management components to WorldCat Local, stating its ambition to be 'continuing the progress toward the truly next generation of library services'.

The OCLC service will support library management for print, electronic and licensed material built on a new, web-scale architecture that is designed to provide 'streamlined workflows and cooperative solutions'. As with ARROW, these co-operative services seek to provide solutions that will enable joint functionality within disparate systems.

2.1.5   The Géant Project

The Géant Project is a collaboration between thirty-four National Research and Education Networks (NRENs) across Europe, the European Commission and DANTE. DANTE is the project's co-ordinating partner.

The Géant Project's founding purpose was to improve the previous TEN-155 pan-European research network by creating a new backbone at gigabit speeds – the Géant network. This network became fully operational at the end of 2001.

GÉANT

Géant now has 12Gbps connectivity to North America and 2.5Gbps to Japan. Additional connections to Géant have been established to the Southern Mediterranean through the EUMEDCONNECT project. Work has also been carried out to establish additional connections to Géant for NRENs from other world regions, including Latin America (through ALICE) and the Asia Pacific region (through TEIN2).

Connected to the Géant network is NORDUnet, a research network used by the Nordic countries (Sweden, Denmark, Norway, Finland and Iceland).

The third phase of the Géant Project started early in 2009, and will last until 2013. The previous parts of the project were mainly focused on building the high capacity network itself. Now that this infrastructure has been completed, it will concentrate on developing and rolling out tools and services to enable the research and education community to get the best performance possible from the network.

There are many European e-learning initiatives that take advantage of these networks. Some of the main ones are listed at: www.elearningeuropa.info/main/index.php?page=fix&id=20

2.1.6   CISAER[148]

CISAER is a project supported by the European Leonardo da Vinci programme. The project aims to provide a comprehensive, state-of-the-art survey of course provision on the Internet, with professional analysis, balanced evaluation and far-reaching recommendations which will provide the field of vocational education and training in the EU with a tool for dealing with this new training dimension.

---

148 www.nettskolen.com/in_english/cisaer

2.2   Higher Education in Europe

In Part One of this report, it was stated that Higher Education still offers the most important market for academic e-book publishers. Table 2.1 illustrates the numbers of new entrants to higher education in the OECD member countries for the years 2004 – 2007[149].

Table 2.1: Numbers of new students in HEI in OECD countries 2004 - 2007

Country	2004	2005	2006	2007
Australia	194,708	231,510	240,424	251,509
Austria	37,718	38,005	41,234	42,693
Belgium	42,552	42,117	44,254	38,196
Czech Republic	53,723	58,007	69,251	74,188
Denmark	34,378	35,379	36,354	35,690
Finland	49,264	48,623	49,874	45,806
Germany	363,123	348,586	341,639	334,808
Greece	44,375	56,194	65,053	57,289
Hungary	95,200	93,402	90,285	84,209
Iceland	3,371	3,139	3,332	3,149
Ireland	28,232	28,332	24,746	27,112
Italy	338,036	342,678	334,650	315,133
Japan	618,283	612,531	617,850	616,950
Korea	365,692	363,920	374,392	388,423
Mexico	578,377	582,849	606,164	630,946
Netherlands	111,407	116,497	115,540	119.658
New Zealand	51,928	46,210	42,552	46,085
Norway	39,523	43,499	39,302	39,521
Poland	461,516	497,060	491,411	474,124
Slovak Republic	41,526	52,005	58,926	62,750
Spain	234,744	226,785	223,566	215,,059
Sweden	86,031	83,810	84,086	82,417
Switzerland	34,913	33,511	34,536	35,894
Turkey	334,197	346,085	393,952	368,383
UK	411,610	410,695	462,921	452,395
USA	2,604,243	2,630,243	2,657,338	2,707,213

NB: No data collected for France, Luxembourg or Portugal.

Source: Organisation for Economic Co-operation and Development (OECD)

149 http://stats.oecd.org/Index.aspx?DatasetCode=RNENTAGE

These figures were compiled by the OECD[150] and are the latest available for the whole group of countries[151]. They should be treated with caution, as the data were almost certainly not supplied on a like-for-like by country basis: some countries have included further education and Vocational Training students in their figures. However, the table nevertheless offers a useful broad guideline to student numbers in Europe and other countries where sales of published products to HEIs are important; and also gives a reliable indication of the countries in which student numbers are growing (or shrinking) most rapidly.

2.3   Opportunities: specific countries

There is much more information available about digital initiatives and opportunities in the Anglophone countries than in Europe and the rest of the world. Some of the sections on European countries below are therefore very short indeed, and amount only to a few notes. This is partly because market statistics on publishing are not as comprehensively collected in some countries as, for example, in the USA and the UK; and partly because (with the possible exception of the Scandinavian countries), the production and selling of digital publications is not as advanced.

In the meantime, it holds true that in mainland Europe, as indeed in the USA and UK, the most lucrative opportunities for selling digital publications currently exist within the HEI library sector. The most effective way for publishers to approach HEI libraries is through their consortia since the majority of HEI libraries belong to at least one consortium, some to several. As also mentioned previously, consortia understand the power that they hold, and will often use it, either individually or collectively (with varying degrees of reasonableness from the publisher's point of view). The International Coalition of Library Consortia (ICOLC)[152] has recently laid down suggested guidelines for publishers to observe when trading electronic products[153]. Part Three of this report gives a fairly comprehensive listing of the main library purchasing consortia worldwide.

---

150 http://stats.oecd.org/Index.aspx?DatasetCode=RGRADSTY
151 There have been no figures collected for France since 2003.
152 www.library.yale.edu/consortia
153 www.library.yale.edu/consortia/statement.html

In some regions – for example, in Eastern Europe, the Middle East and parts of Asia – it is almost impossible for publishers to penetrate the institutional market in countries where they do not have a direct representative, unless they use an agent[154]. In certain countries, local agents are the most effective. Some publishers prefer to use one of the big international agencies, such as EBSCO[155] or SWETs[156] (both of which are now active in the promotion of e-books). A third option is to contact the director(s) of one or more consortia in the country concerned. They are often administrators or managers rather than librarians, and may be prepared either to act on behalf of the publisher in return for a fee, or suggest a suitable contact willing to perform this service.

2.3.1   USA

Government

Access to a broadband network is essential for the complete integration of ICT within a country's economy, and the American government has long recognised this. Fuelled primarily by private sector investment and innovation, and encouraged by the government, the American broadband ecosystem has evolved rapidly. The number of Americans who had broadband at home grew from eight million in 2000 to nearly 200 million in 2009. However, 100 million American still do not have broadband at home. Therefore, early in 2009 Congress launched its **National Broadband Plan**[157], to ensure that every American has "access to broadband capability." Congress also required that this plan should include a detailed strategy for achieving affordability and maximizing use of broadband to advance "consumer welfare, civic participation, public safety and homeland security, community development, health care delivery, energy independence and efficiency, education, employee training, private sector investment, entrepreneurial activity, job creation and economic growth, and other national purposes."

The plan is a comprehensive programme which addresses every aspect of American society as it is affected by or could be improved by broadband

---

154 Unfortunately there is (as far as I know) at present no comprehensive directory of agents.
155 http://search.ebscohost.com
156 www.swets.com
157 www.broadband.gov/plan

access. The project has six formal goals:

Goal No. 1: At least 100 million US homes should have affordable access to actual download speeds of at least 100 megabits per second and actual upload speeds of at least 50 megabits per second.

Goal No. 2: The USA should lead the world in mobile innovation, with the fastest and most extensive wireless networks of any nation.

Goal No. 3: Every American should have affordable access to robust broadband service, and the means and skills to subscribe if they so choose.

Goal No. 4: Every American community should have affordable access to at least 1 gigabit per second broadband service to anchor institutions such as schools, hospitals and government buildings.

Goal No. 5: To ensure the safety of the American people, every first responder should have access to a nationwide, wireless, interoperable broadband public safety network.

Goal No. 6: To ensure that America leads in the clean energy economy, every American should be able to use broadband to track and manage their real-time energy consumption.

The plan is currently in the beta stage of development. As the project outline acknowledges, trying to establish a completion date is difficult, because continuing I.T. developments will mean that it needs ongoing refinements. However, there seems to be a universal will to make it succeed, and even a partial implementation is bound to benefit academic publishers, since for most the USA represents a large market for their publications.

Retail

The Association of American Publishers (AAP)[158] and the International Digital Publishing Forum (IDPF)[159] each collects e-book sales data in the USA. The IDPF figures relate to trade eBook sales via wholesale channels from a limited number (about 15) of publishers, and therefore do not reflect the whole market. The figures collected by the IDPF for e-book sales in 2002 were US$5.8m and US$165.8m in 2009, representing a 28.5 times increase over the period. The AAP collects figures from a wider group of publishers, but has not been carrying out this activity for as long as the IDPF. The figure that it reported for e-book sales in the USA in 2009 was US$313m, which represented a 176.6 per cent increase on 2008. It should be noted that the AAP's figures reflect publishers' revenues, not the retail value of sales overall. E-book sales in the USA in 2009 still accounted for only approximately 1 per cent of total book sales, which may seem to be an insignificant figure; however, it is the growth rate that is important. Given that book sales in the USA have been 'flat' for several years and the evident migration by consumers from print books to e-books are likely to make e-books an important source of revenue for publishers within a relatively short period of time. As a rule of thumb, it is probably fair to say that the USA is about two years ahead of the UK in consumer adoption and appreciation of e-books (partly because a greater range of both hand-held readers and e-books may be bought there), and that the UK is at least one year ahead of the rest of Europe.

Most American bookselling chains now sell e-books. The main ones are Barnes & Noble; Books-a-Million; Books Inc.; Borders; Deseret Book; Follett's; Joseph-Beth Booksellers; Shakespeare and Co; and Follett's. Online-only booksellers are led by Amazon and Fictionwise. Both ContentReserve (a division of OverDrive) and Ingram Digital offer affordable digital platforms for booksellers.

Schools

Use of computers for learning is widespread in US schools (as in the UK). Most e-books are accessed via tablets or PCs, but there are already some

---

158 www.publishers.org
159 www.idpf.org

initiatives in place to introduce hand-held readers to the classroom[160]. More schools material in e-book format is available in the USA than in other countries. Publishers seeking to capitalise on this market will probably find that partnering with one of the aggregators that specialise in solutions for schools will be most effective. These include Follett's[161], who claim to be able to offer access to more than 60,000 schools, and Vital Source [162].

An important opportunity for publishers wishing to introduce their publications into US schools is provided by the US's National Instructional Materials Accessibility Standard[163] (NIMAS) legislation, which was introduced in 2004, and is roughly the equivalent of the UK's SENDA[164] legislation.

NIMAS has been summarised thus:

> *"The Secretary of Education has authorized OSEP, The Office of Special Education Programs, to issue a supplement to the National Center on Accessing the General Curriculum led by CAST, to convene an expert panel to establish a voluntary national standard for accessible digital instructional materials for students with disabilities. This new standard basically mandates that all K-12 textbooks be produced by publishers in NIMAS format in addition to the traditional print format."*

Overwhelmingly, publishers are choosing to observe the NIMAS legislation by producing their publications in suitable digital format, because the alternatives are often unwieldy, expensive and not necessarily accessible by readers with certain types of disability (though electronic formats do not cater for all disadvantaged readers, and some publications – e.g., those relating to some scientific subjects or containing tables or complex diagrams – may be too difficult or too costly to digitise).

---

160 A list of handheld readers suitable for use in US elementary and secondary schools may be found at: www.k12open-ed.com/products.php?sectionname=software.
161 www.fdr.follett.com
162 http://vitalsource.com
163 www.gh-accessibility.com/legislation/nimas-legislative.php
164 www.opsi.gov.uk/acts/acts2001/ukpga_20010010_en_1

Public libraries

The USA has more than 9,000 public libraries. In 2007, the most recent year for which statistics are available, these libraries together offered 207,551 public-use Internet accessible computers on their premises and held an average of 1,428.1 electronic books[165]. This equates to 13.2m items held in total. 10.7% of total expenditure by public libraries is on electronic materials (electronic books, databases and electronic subscriptions). A breakdown of the type of electronic books purchased is not available, but the greater part of these items were almost certainly audiobooks, though interest in e-books has existed for some years in US public libraries and is increasing. Obviously it would be unfeasible for publishers to approach American public libraries individually, because sales would be too small; but by placing their e-books with the main aggregators, especially NetLibrary, MyiLibrary, EBL and Ebrary, and by working with OverDrive, which saw the potential offered by the US public library service very early on, this lucrative and growing market can be tapped efficiently. Big publishers with large e-book collections may also be able to sell them to library consortia in the US. American library consortia (of which there are many more than anywhere else in the world) differ from those in other countries by often being regionally based, rather than grouped according to the educational or social sector in which they operate. (See also Part Three.)

Academic libraries

By far the biggest opportunities for selling digital products in the US, as elsewhere in the world, exist within the HE sector. Although, in common with HE libraries almost everywhere, North American university libraries claim to be feeling the pinch of the 'double whammy' of funds not keeping pace with inflation and the ever-burgeoning list of demands on their budgets, by the standards of the rest of the world they are extremely wealthy. It has been estimated that 80 per cent of all HE library sales by revenue take place in North America (that is, the USA and Canada together).

---

165 This information has been taken from the ALA public library statistics report for 2007 (published 2009), which may be found at http://harvester.census.gov/imls/pubs/pls/pub_detail.asp?id=122#

The best source of information on the extent of electronic sales in this sector is the Association of Research Libraries[166] (ARL), which for many years has collected annual statistics[167] and performance indicators for a group of 123 elite research libraries serving HE institutions in the USA and Canada (the Canadian members of the Association are relatively few in number). ARL statistics are therefore not exclusively for the US, nor do they provide comprehensive information about the whole North American academic sector; but they do give accurate year-on-year information on expenditure by the most prestigious and therefore best-endowed libraries, as well as indicating trends for the sector as a whole.

In the academic year 2007/08, the last year for which a complete set of ARL statistics is available, expenditure by the ARL libraries on 'computer files – one time monographic purchase' (i.e., e-books bought outright on a book-by-book basis rather than as part of a licensed collection or database) totalled US$73.1m, up 22.2 per cent on 2006/07. 2006/07 was the first year that electronic monographs were split out from other types of electronic resource within the statistics, so it is not possible to calculate by how much expenditure on them increased in that year from 2005 - 2006; but the following note[168] gives an indication:

> *"Not only have electronic materials expenditures grown sharply in the past decade, they have grown at a rate far exceeding that of library materials expenditure overall ...the average ARL university library now spends just under 47 per cent of its materials budget on electronic materials (N.B. this figure includes journals) ... and 50 ARL libraries report that they spend more than 50 per cent of their materials budget on electronic materials."*

This information is not only of significance to publishers wishing to sell e-books to the US HE market, but also extremely important to those publishers that are either already selling or planning to sell electronic books and electronic journals on the same platform, or who are making longer term plans to sell 'content' as opposed to format-specific publications.

---

166 www.arl.org
167 The statistics may be found at www.arl.org/stats/annualsurveys/arlstats/arlstats07.shtml
168 ARL Statistics 2006 – 2007, p. 18.

It is worth pointing out that, because library budgets remain static or are actually in decline in terms of buying power, the increased commitment of funds to e-books is taking place at the expense of both print books and journals expenditure, reversing the situation of only a few years ago, when e-books were typically paid for out of one-off 'seed-corn' budgets or as part of an end-of-year 'spending up' exercise. In other words, e-book purchase has progressed from being experimental to mainstream, and is well on its way to becoming second only to the purchase of journals as an item in resources budget expenditure. The prominence accorded to e-books is being aided by the provision of better usage statistics, and the greater attention being paid to them by librarians anxious to demonstrate that they are providing value for money. As a result, librarians no longer regard journals as the sacred cows of their budgeting process, and they are increasingly likely to cancel subscriptions to journals that are not being used by their patrons and/or demand more flexibility within the 'big deal' journals bundles provided by publishers and subscription agents.

This is not to say that US HE librarians are not demanding when it comes to e-book purchase. They are constantly seeking innovations from suppliers as they become accustomed to the format. This means that publishers need to be conversant with the requirements of the particular consortia that they wish to deal with - America has almost as many library purchasing consortia as the rest of the world put together - and sometimes of individual libraries, before choosing their aggregator partners or planning innovations to their platforms. For example, some may require e-books to be made available through an interlibrary loan system, such as the one set up between MyiLibrary and CISTI in 2007[169].

The most sophisticated consortia – which are often also the ones most aggressive in their demands – may ask publishers and aggregators to provide e-books on the proprietary platforms that they have developed for consortium members. OhioLink[170] is the very powerful consortium of more than eighty libraries of all types in the State of Ohio that has pioneered this concept. Despite misgivings, many large publishers have now acquiesced to the requirement. Other consortia are likely to follow OhioLink's lead.

---

169 See http://cat.cisti-icist.nrc-cnrc.gc.ca/search
170 www.ohiolink.edu

However, the rewards can be great. Some of the wealthiest American universities and consortia are now investing in huge ongoing collections of e-books, sometimes supplied through a single aggregator who has been awarded the business on a contractual basis, sometimes by dealing with several parties including publishers who can supply e-books via their own platforms. Several of the big university libraries are experimenting with 'patron select' or ' instant purchase' e-book models, which involve allowing patrons to see details about all of the titles available from an aggregator or publisher, even the ones that the library has not purchased: if an unpurchased title scores an agreed number of 'hits', the library automatically purchases it. At the other end of the scale, publishers report that 'do-it-yourself' compilations, individual chapter sales and book or chapter time-limited rentals are becoming increasingly popular. There are also many opportunities available to publishers through platforms geared more specifically to pedagogical requirements, such CourseSmart, Vital Source and various VLEs.

2.3.2   Canada

Government

Canada does not at present have a national digital strategy, but there is accelerating lobbying of the government to produce one. The Canadian government has, however, already spent considerable resource on developing and funding Canarie[171], Canada's advanced research and innovation network. Established in 1993, it is a non-profit corporation that serves over 50,000 researchers at almost 200 Canadian universities and colleges, government labs, research institutes, hospitals and other private and public sector organisations, and connects them to innovators across the country and around the world. Canarie provides advanced networking capability that enables scientists to manage, analyse and exchange very large volumes of data, sometimes leading to ground-breaking discoveries. It also enables researchers and their partners to develop new tools that harness the power of the network; for example, it has carried out important work on using technologies to reduce carbon emissions and help slow the rate of climate change. Many of the organisations which belong to Canarie are large customers for online publications.

---

171 www.canarie.ca

Retail[172]

Canada, of course, has two languages, English and French. However, the Canadian market for digital book content is largely shaped by international publishing companies, which means that most of the e-books available are English-language publications (though in the HE market the aggregator Numilog, which offers both English and French titles, is prominent). Canadian-owned publishing companies have been slow to publish digital editions of their books, probably because most of them are relatively small. For audiobooks, there are three established publishing programmes in English Canada, and nine in French Canada. Together, English and French audiobook sales were estimated to total CA$7.5m – CA$10.5m in 2008. There are no available statistics for e-book sales, but it has been estimated that the Canadian market has followed roughly the same pattern as the US market. In 2006, Canadian book sales for the consumer market were estimated at CA$1.2bn. In the USA during the same period, e-book sales were estimated to represent 1 per cent of total book sales. If this held true for the Canadian market, total e-book sales in Canada will then have been about CA$1.2m.

Outlets for digital publications, especially for audiobooks[173], are well-developed in Canada; and its 'porous' relationship with the USA means that e-books can easily be sourced online both from bricks-and-mortar and online booksellers operating in the US. The main Canadian bookshop chains are Archambault, Book Warehouse, Chapters, Coles, Follett of Canada, Indigo, Librairie Raffin, McNally Robinson, Nicholas Hoare and Renaud Bray. A comprehensive listing of all bricks-and-mortar and online booksellers operating in Canada may be found at: http://canadabooksellers.com/.

---

172 Much of the information in this section is taken from the report Audiobook and eBook publishing in Canada, prepared for Library and Archives Canada by Turner-Riggs in October 2008. www.collectionscanada.gc.ca/obj/005002/f2/005002-2100-e.pdf

173 Turner-Riggs says: Québec Amérique and Planète rebelle are distributed by Prologue, and Les Éditions ATMA international by Les Messageries ADP in Quebec and by DG Diffusion in France. Les Éditions AdA and L'Oeil qui écoute distribute directly to bookstores, while Les Éditions un monde different and Alexandre Stanké use Agence MSH, a distributor specialising in audio titles. Alexandre Stanké has a particularly highly developed network, also employing the Quebec electronic platform iThèque and France's Daudin, Belgium's La Caravelle, and Switzerland's Servidis-Transat in foreign markets, and having established business relations with Audible.fr.

Schools

Canada has been a great innovator and experimenter with using online resources for education – perhaps because, like Australia, it has a relatively small population which occupies a huge geographical area. SchoolNet was a partnership between Canada's provincial and territorial governments, the education community and the private sector. It was set up in 1999 to promote the effective use of information technologies in learning. The SchoolNet partnership connected Canada's schools and public libraries to the Internet in the same year – a global first. By May 2000, there were almost half a million connected computers in Canadian schools. By 2005, the Canadian government had built on these two initiatives by establishing approximately 10,000 public Internet access sites in rural, remote and urban communities (the UK People's Network initiative is similar in philosophy).

At the end of June 2007, SchoolNet was wound up, and has been superseded by a range of other more sophisticated, more targeted initiatives that have been developed to promote the use of online resources in schools and other educational institutions and virtual communities. Statistics Canada lists learning resources for teachers which provide useful information for publishers seeking to enter the market[174].

As well as having become an integral part of conventional secondary and further education in Canada, online resources are used exclusively by a relatively high number of students at all educational levels.

In 2004, there were 5,000 students of school age in Canada who were enrolled in virtual schools offering a complete education via the Internet.

Public libraries

Canadian public libraries, by virtue of the country's constitution, are governed by the provinces rather than the state. However, a number of important digital initiatives have taken place over the past decade, and have meant that they have worked in partnership for much of the time and bid jointly for funding for large projects.

---

174 www.statcan.gc.ca/edu/edu01_0000-eng.htm

Canada's public libraries are listed at:
www.collectionscanada.gc.ca/gateway/s22-212-e.html.

Academic Libraries

Please refer to the ARL figures and other information in the US Higher Education in section 2.3.1.

The Canadian Virtual University[175] is a consortium of 12 universities that offers more than 2,300 courses and 300 programmes, of which several hundred are delivered entirely online. In 2006, 115,000 students were registered with the CVU.

A list of Canada' universities can be found at:
http://offshorewave.com/universities_listed_by_Country/Universities_in_
Canada.html.

2.3.3   UK

Government

In January 2009, the UK government published Digital Britain: an Interim Report, for consultation. The final version of the report was published in June 2009 and an implementation plan issued in August 2009[176]. The proposals from the report helped to create the Digital Economy Bill, which was debated in Parliament in the last days of the Labour government and became the Digital Economy Act.

The *Digital Economy Act 2010*[177], which was passed in the final days of the Labour administration in April 2010, contains several important measures which will affect publishers. The most significant of these is the so-called 'three strikes' rule, which provides OFCOM with new powers to control digital infringement of copyright amongst both pirate sites and individuals who download illegal content. A code of conduct is currently being consulted on to regulate this legislation, but the headline where

---

175 www.cvu-uvc.ca
176 www.culture.gov.uk/images/publications/digitalbritain-finalreport-jun09.pdf
177 www.opsi.gov.uk/acts/acts2010/pdf/ukpga_20100024_en.pdf

illegal content is found to have been uploaded or downloaded, rights holders may work with Internet Service Providers (ISPs) on removing this content and taking action against those responsible. Specific connections (IP addresses) which are found to have accessed illegal content will be reported to the ISP which provides the Internet connection, and copyright infringement notices will be sent out from rights holders via the ISPs to the subscribers responsible. Ultimately, if those subscribers do not take action to stop copyright infringement from their connection after a series of notices being issued, rights holders will be able to apply to the courts to take legal action against them for the infringement. The Act also contains a clause which would enable the Secretary of State to enact legislation to sever the Internet connections of copyright infringers, but this would only take effect should the OFCOM-regulated legislation not be successful in reducing copyright infringement.

Of greater significance to booksellers than publishers, but still important, is the Act's extension of the Public Lending Right to e-books and audio books. This provision applies to books used on the library premises and loaned for use off the premises (e.g. on CD or memory stick), but specifically excludes any items being sent to the borrower electronically. This extension of PLR retains the requirement that libraries should not lend out works for commercial gain.

E-book statistics

The Publishers Association began collecting data on UK publishers' digital[178] sales for the first time in 2008, with figures provided by companies whose physical book sales represent c60 per cent of the total for all UK publishers. This exercise was repeated in 2009, with participation increasing to companies whose physical book sales represented around two-thirds of the total in both years Table 2.2 indicates only the amalgamated sales of the companies supplying the data, and has not been 'grossed up' from actual sales figures in the way that sales data on print books are.

---

178 'Digital' here refers to electronic publications only; it does not include print books produced by POD technologies.

Table 2.2: Amagalmated sales from PA's all sector digital survey 2008-2009

£m	Total	General consumer	Consumer reference	School/ELT	Academic/ professional
2008	78.2	1.2	4.4	9.0	63.6
2009	93.7	3.6	5.4	7.3	77.4
2008/2009 % change	+19.9	+190.0	+22.0	-18.1	+21.7

NB: Figures for companies supplying data only

Source: PA Statistics Yearbook 2009, The Publishers Association, April 2010

The PA therefore emphasises that this data should be treated with caution "given the exploratory nature of the collection and the potential within this new area for inconsistencies in the way that the companies define and record their digital sales. The PA's commentary is as follows:

> *"Given that the companies providing digital sales data accounted for c67 per cent of the physical book sales of all UK publishers and taking into account the balance of participants in terms of category published,we might roughly calculate that* **total UK publisher sales of digital products in 2009 would be around just over £150m**, *split approximately £5m general consumer, £8m consumer reference, £8-9m school/ELT and £130m academic/professional.*
>
> *Digital sales worth £150m would represent around 4-5 per cent of the combined physical and digital sales of UK publishers in 2009, although that proportion would vary between around 13 per cent of sales in the academic/ professional sector, 2 per cent of school/ELT, and less than 1 per cent of sales of consumer titles.*
>
> *While the digital sales survey asked respondents to provide unit sales figures in this sector, in addition to the value figures indicated above, it is clear that the measure of a 'unit' is not necessarily applicable to the way that digital products are sold, particularly in the consumer reference, school/ELT and academic/ professional sectors, where much of the revenue for digital sales comes from subscriptions providing access*

to online material or e-books. However, in the general consumer sector (i.e. where most reported digital sales were of e-books or audiobook downloads), the 'unit' measure remains a useful way to analyse sales. The reported unit sales of general consumer digital products from the companies supplying data were a little over 0.7m in 2009, around three times the figure for 2008. The average invoiced unit price for these consumer products was £4.90 in 2009, down 4 per cent on 2008 (£5.11). These average prices were higher than those for physical books in the combined consumer (fiction, non-fiction/reference and children's) categories (£2.92 in 2009, down from £2.84 in 2008)."

Retail

All of the main UK bookshop chains now sell e-books from transactional websites. W.H. Smith was the first: e-books have now been available from its website for more than a decade[179]. Waterstone's and Borders sell them for uploading on the Sony e-book reader[180]; Blackwell's offers an e-book service in partnership with Taylor & Francis[181]; and John Smith campus bookshops sell e-books in a range of formats[182]. Some of the large independents, such as Foyle's[183], also provide an e-book service. Certain aggregators, such as ebooks.com (the retail arm of EBL) and Knovel, have developed a retail solution which publishers can partner. An increasing number of publishers are selling e-books to the retail sector from their own platforms. For those too small to do so, or not ready yet to launch their own service, Gardner's offers a range of options which are both effective and affordable[184].The already-established influence of the Internet upon retailing as a whole and the retail book industry in

179 http://ebooks.whsmith.co.uk/830E0058-0151-4E4F-9427-D4B53F6A0946/10/132/en/Help-FAQ-Format410.htm
180 www.waterstones.com/waterstonesweb/browse/ebooks/4294964587/;
http://ebooks.borders.com/content/borders/index.shtml
181 http://blackwell.etailer.dpsl.net/Home/html/index.asp
182 www.jscampus.co.uk/shop/text.asp?mscssid=.&P=ebooks
183 www.foyles.co.uk/help/help_ebooks.asp?CID=
184 www.gardners.com/gardners/include.aspx?l=/gardners/content/Retailers/Digital_Warehouse/intro.htm

particular will undoubtedly accelerate consumer adoption of e-books once user-friendly, affordable hand-held devices are commonly available. A Mintel report published in 2009 found that in 2008, 73 per cent of all households had ordered goods by Internet, phone or post for delivery, with 37 per cent receiving deliveries at least monthly, compared to just 64 per cent and 27 per cent respectively in 2002.

The *Reading the Future* survey undertaken by *The Next Big Thing* towards the end of 2009 found that 33 per cent of respondents (from a sample of 3,159) thought that an easy-to-read electronic book reader sounded appealing, and 26.5 per cent would like to be able to download a book on to their mobile or iPad. The same survey found that people who buy books online are the lead group which likes e-readers (33.8 per cent). Yet, the report continues, "they are in a statistical dead heat, with people who buy in chains (33.7 per cent) and independent bookshops (33.7 per cent) …. the results show an increasing acceptance of technology among people who buy in the traditional bricks-and-mortar shops. Indie and chain buyers are particularly keen on POD machines (40.7 per cent and 40.5 per cent)". 46 per cent of the people surveyed said that they would be persuaded to buy an e-book if downloadable books cost less than 'normal' books, and 43 per cent said that they would buy one if it was as easy to read on a handheld reader as it was to read a print book. These percentages are impressive when it is taken into account that the respondents were mostly not early adopters, but discussing concepts of which they had no first-hand experience.

Some of the statistics released by publishers themselves are even more extreme. About two years after Harlequin, Mills & Boon launched its e-book site, it conducted an online survey of its readers which attracted 4,020 responses.[185] 50.7 per cent of these were from people who bought e-books. 80 per cent of all the respondents used the 'Search Inside the Book' widget on the Mills & Boon website. 18.7 per cent said that they read more than 10 books a month, and 11.6 per cent said that they read more than 10 e-books per month. 22.7 per cent said that they read at least one e-book per month. 44 per cent of those who bought e-books

185 The number of responses was in itself impressive, though not every respondent answered every question. HMB kindly made the raw data available to me in March 2010. A full analysis of all the findings has yet to be completed.

bought them from HMB's own website – that HMB scored the highest figure here is not surprising, given the nature of the survey. However, 24.3 per cent also bought e-books from ebooks.com; 21.7 per cent from waterstones.com; 17.4 per cent from WHSmith.com; 18 per cent from the Amazon 'Kindle' ebookstore; 5.2 per cent from tesco.com; and 22.6 per cent bought them, but from 'none of these'. It should be added that Mills & Boon has created a particularly attractive e-book proposition for its readers, to receive the full benefit of which they have to commit to regular purchases. Its publishing model, which depends on monthly releases in each of its sub-genres, and in some ways has more in common with the magazine market than with traditional book publishing, lends itself to this. Nevertheless, these figures reveal that a consumer swing from print to electronic can take place very rapidly indeed.

Schools

For traditional educational publishers (most of whom offer digital products), the best way of keeping up with the demands of what is a complex and contradictory digital market in UK schools is through the Educational Publishing Council (EPC), the schools division of The Publishers Association. The Council invites speakers from all the government quangos and agencies that deliver educational policy to give regular updates to its members. At present, digital-only publishers and educational software providers are not members of the EPC. Most of them belong to a sub-group of the British Educational Suppliers Association (BESA) known as the Educational Software Publishers Association (ESPA)[186].

Curriculum Online (COL)[187] was funded by the Department of Education and Skills (DfES) and managed by BECTA[188] to provide a search and discovery mechanism for digital learning products for teachers. However, funding for both this and BECTA has now been withdrawn, and no new material is being posted to the site. In 2009 BECTA published its 'Harnessing Technology' guidelines for schools[189]. The TEEM[190] and

---

186 www.besanet.org.uk/besa/bytopic/topic.jsp?topic=48
187 www.curriculumonline.gov.uk
188 www.becta.org.uk
189 http://publications.becta.org.uk/display.cfm?resID=39754
190 www.teem.org.uk

Schoolzone[191] websites both offer a peer-reviewed service for educational software packages.

The government also sponsored a Content Advisory Board (CAB) as part of the Curriculum Online initiative. Its work has now been archived – information about this can be found on the BECTA website. Its reports offered publishers and other interested parties a short-cut to understanding new developments in the digital learning market, and some of the archived material is still useful for this purpose.

Some of the figures quoted in its reports are interesting, because they demonstrate that a close approximation of the 20/80 rule has hitherto applied to this market. Thus, despite the existence in COL of 800 digital suppliers to UK schools and 15,000 digital products, the top ten suppliers have 50 per cent of the market and the top 25 have 75 per cent. The 'long tail' is therefore even longer in the digital learning/educational software market than in other sectors of the publishing industry.

In the state education sector, funded by an annual government fund £100m from 2002–2008 spending on digital products was resourced by a system of electronic learning credits. However, owing to the parallel government move of allowing individual schools to take more responsibility for their budgets, there is compelling evidence that although this money was ring-fenced in theory, in practice schools were not necessarily spending it on electronic resources. Nevertheless, the total value of the market is still probably about £70m[192]; but the educational print market is still worth at least twice as much as the educational digital market. This is a reversal of the situation in the higher education library market, where the print market now represents a fraction of the electronic market, and the electronic market is increasing its percentage of resource significantly every year. Yet nearly all schools have smartboards and other sophisticated hardware provided by government funding; and UK schools are arguably now better-equipped digitally than schools in any other country in the world, because of the advantages they have gained from twelve years of targeted

191 www.schoolzone.co.uk
192 The discrepancy between this and the figures supplied by the PA in the E-books statistics in Table 2.2 can be explained by the fact that the largest suppliers of digital resources to schools are 'non-traditional' – i.e., not from the established publishers from whom the PA collected the figures.

government initiatives. Some schools are better equipped electronically than some universities, and almost all are better equipped than the average FE college. Over time, therefore, the transition from mainly print to mainly electronic learning resources in schools looks inevitable.

The top twenty products in the educational digital market take 40 per cent of the total revenue for this market. This is broadly comparable with print. Popular materials increase their rate of adoption by word of mouth. In terms of subject profile, 30 per cent is spent on ICT, both as a subject and on products underpinning the use of IT in schools; English, Maths and Science products take 60 per cent of the market, of which Science has 10 per cent or less; and all other subjects account for the remaining 10 per cent (or less).

Of the top fifteen companies with the greatest market share, the biggest player is Research Machines[193], which enjoys about one third of the total spend. After them comes a company called R-E-M[194] which strictly speaking is a distributor of educational products. After these (in no particular order) are Crocodile Clips[195]: scientific materials; Espresso Education, which offers a product that involves downloading material from satellites[196]; Immerse Education[197]; Logotron[198]; Sherston[199]; Tag Learning[200]; and Granada Learning[201]. Also in the frame are the established publishers who also offer digital products. Key ones are Harcourt[202], HarperCollins, OUP, CUP, Hodder and Nelson Thornes.

Overall, Research Machines is the biggest company in the UK educational resource market. It supplies networks, hardware and enabling software. Taking it out of the equation, the rest of the market consists of what is

193 known as RM – see www.rm.com
194 www.r-e-m.co.uk/cgi-bin/xrem
195 www.crocodile-clips.com
196 www.espresso.co.uk
197 www.immersioneducation.co.uk/
198 www.logotron.co.uk/
199 www2.sherston.com/default.aspx
200 www.taglearning.com/index.php
201 www.granada-learning.com
202 Now a Pearson imprint

virtually a 50/50 split between the established publishers and the digital-only companies. This includes the very long tail of companies with either a small product or a small customer base, particularly in digital supply.

Few of these products export well as they stand. Some of the tools and underlying packages might be exportable, although, just as in the UK, they would still have to be aligned very closely to local educational practice and curriculum requirements.

The sales statistics available are product-orientated, not channel-orientated. However, these are incomplete and unreliable, because for the most part suppliers are selling direct to schools and not through intermediaries such as direct purchasing organisations (DPOs), even though these constitute a major supply channel for non-technical goods.

There are some challenges in the area of ICT which have existed since the first products began to be developed more than 20 years ago, and which have yet to be addressed. These are:

- There is **no satisfactory demonstration mechanism**. If schools are interested in a book, they can telephone for an inspection copy. There is no similar viable method in place for electronic products. Because of the federal nature of schools, there are real problems in providing samples that reach all the decision-makers and potential users, and similar problems in setting up an adequate marketing channel.

- Schools are **not using any kind of systematic product appraisal system**. They buy materials from catalogues or from sales representatives, or by ordering as a result of recommendations from colleagues or peers in other schools.

- It was originally believed that digitised content would increase granularity, and make small amounts of material available to teachers quickly – for example, a teacher preparing a lesson on the Battle of Hastings might be able to download some information about it the night before the lesson. However, this does not work in practice because **schools do not have an approved method of paying online**. All but the most insignificant payments have to be made by cheque, often with two signatures. Until this problem is cracked, the market will be driven by a relatively small number of packages that do not depend on time-sensitive delivery.

- **What any supplier is up against with schools is their innate conservatism,** their need to spend their money very wisely indeed, and their reluctance to be first with any new product.

- **State schools are probably a better bet initially,** as they are more inclined to use I.T. products than independent schools, though the latter often have more money to spend. However, It is important to note that all the statistics available relate to the state sector. The independent sector represents a separate opportunity, though it is even more fragmented, because it has no unifying central influences such as state directives or local authorities.

- **Segmentation of the market is vital** to make a clear distinction between what is on offer for primary schools, secondary schools, sixth form colleges and tertiary colleges. A one-size-fits-all product would almost certainly not work.

Based on the above information, and bearing in mind the curriculum and syllabus changes that took place in the school year 2008/09, which meant that most of the state schools' materials budgets had to be spent on print books, it is, however, suggested that this market may now be opening up again. The backward trend is almost certain to be reversed eventually and the local issues identified in the last section will be resolved over time. How quickly the reversal will happen, and to what extent electronic learning materials will replace traditional ones, will depend partly on the conclusions that educational psychologists reach about the effectiveness and safety of online learning for younger children, and, if it is found to be effective and safe, how much of it is appropriate; and, more generally, the educational policy of the current Coalition government, which at the time of writing has yet to be announced.

Schools are best approached individually by publishers, though some schools operating within the same local authority work very closely with each other and may have formed groups which purchase collectively. Some make purchases through Direct Purchasing Organisations (DPOs) run by their local authorities. Secondary schools now frequently apply to be recognised as specialists in particular disciplines – for example, ICT, Sport, Languages, Science and the Arts. Discovering the specialism(s) of a particular school is obviously helpful to publishers hoping to sell to it specific types of publication. School libraries hold budgets which are normally divided up between the different subjects taught by the school. Many large schools now have dedicated librarians, and some few are beginning to appoint digital librarians, or, if they can not afford this, a librarian with experience in purchasing and using online resources.

Public libraries

The question of what can be charged for is crucial in assessing UK public libraries' speed of adoption of e-books. Should they be able to charge for loaning them in the same way that they charge for other electronic products, or does the same embargo apply to them as to print books? And if it is decided that libraries can charge, how in practice would it work? This debate is still taking place.

Perhaps partly for these reasons, partly because of funding pressures, e-books have yet to form part of mainstream public library expenditure in the UK, except in a few well-publicised instances. Recent e-book projects have included Co-East, a joint initiative between Loughborough University and Essex Public Libraries that was funded by the LASER Foundation, and involved the purchase of 12 handheld readers for loan to members of the public, who could then use them to access titles from Coutts/ Ebrary[203] and OverDrive; an experiment by Blackburn with Darwen public library service to lend out 40 PDAs that could then be loaded with titles from OverDrive; and an initiative by the London Borough of Richmond to make available e-audio recordings plus e-books from NetLibrary and Safari available to borrowers via PCs. In Essex and Richmond, these projects have resulted in the permanent purchase of e-books as part of the library's regular spend. How far and how quickly other libraries will follow suit depends on the demographics of individual library services (the library e-book clientele so far has comprised young people aged 18-24,

---

203 This was prior to the launch of the MyiLibrary platform.

senior citizens, those with mobility difficulties, and library reading groups); and the impact of the People's Network: and possible pending government legislation on whether or not e-books should be lent free of charge (see Section 2.1.1).

The People's Network[204]

Electronic services through public libraries have been given a huge boost by the People's Network. The People's Network was a brainchild of the Blair Administration in the early, idealistic period of its first term. The People's Network website describes itself as follows:

> *The People's Network is your network, whoever you are, whatever it is you want to do. It is delivered by England's public libraries, managed by the Museums, Libraries and Archives Council (www.mla.gov.uk) and supported by lottery funding.*
>
> *People's Network services started with computers in public libraries giving high speed access to the web for everyone. In total the network in libraries offers over 60 million hours of computer use every year, most of it free, with access to a wide range of software and digital content, in buildings already rich with collections of books and other material, all supported by trained and supportive staff[205] .*

The government's stated agenda for the People's Network is that it should encourage digital skills and 24/7 access to the Internet for all; that it should give people access free of charge to "websites, portals, virtual reference, community information, e-content (e.g., online reference, e-books and audio)." A search on the People's Network brings up links to 1,015,554[206] 'resources', including many sites that offer e-books. Many of these can not be accessed directly through the People's Network, but describe where the resources are located and how to access them. A high proportion of

204 www.peoplesnetwork.gov.uk
205 www.questionpoint.org/crs/servlet/org.oclc.home.TFSRedirect?virtcategory=10836
206 Information recorded on 1st July 2010.

of the entries relates to local history archive materials, photographic collections, etc.; e-content, therefore, rather than discrete e-texts. However, the publicisation of these free resources is likely over time to encourage demand for commercially-produced e-publications from public libraries.

In 2008 OCLC, then the owners of NetLibrary, conducted a survey of UK public libraries which indicated that 50 per cent of them intended to increase their collections of audiobooks and e-books over the following twelve months.   These findings encouraged OCLC to develop a 'starter pack' for public libraries. For one flat fee (including access) of $6,000, the libraries could offer their users a collection of more than 40 e-audiobooks and more than 150 e-books from NetLibrary. The starter pack covered a wide variety of genres and front list titles that had been specifically handpicked to appeal to UK public library users. If the library could not afford this initial outlay, it could purchase either the e-book starter pack or the e-audiobook starter pack (including access) for $3,000[207]. Ebrary has just launched a similar service[208] . Such initiatives offer publishers a relatively trouble-free way of entering the public library market with e-books.

A few publishers have succeeded in promoting their own e-book collections to public libraries.   For example, some of OUP's online collections are licensed extensively within the sector. OUP says that the key to success with public libraries is to devoted significant investment to training programmes for librarians and to create financial models that are attractive to the sector.

In common with other kinds of library, public libraries purchase a great deal through consortia (see Section Three). There are also special interest groups for librarians which publishers can contact as appropriate to promote their content[209].

---

207   www.oclc.org/uk/en/enews/2009/10/en_econtent.htm
208   http://newsbreaks.infotoday.com/NewsBreaks/Public-Library-Complete-PLC-from-ebrary-
        Offers-Ebooks-and-More-67579.asp
209   www.cilip.org.uk/specialinterestgroups/bysubject

Academic libraries

Table 2.3 sets out expenditure on resources by UK HEI libraries over the past four years, and Figure 2.1 shows the expenditure on electronic resources (excluding serials) in percentage terms.

Table 2.3: Expenditure by UK university libraries 2004/05-2007/08

£'000	2004/05	2005;/06	2006/07	2007/08	% change 2004/05 - 2007/08
Books and non-book materials	50,355	52,504	52,392	51,176	+2%
+/- previous	-0.4%	4.6%	-0.2%	2.3%	
Journals	96,192	102,176	113,678	112,678	+17.1%
+/- previous	+2.1%	+6.2%	+11.3%	-0.9%	
Electronic items*	27,620	32,414	39,391	38,873	+40.7%
+/- previous	+11.7%	+17.3%	+21.5%	-1.3%	
Total	173,988	187,094	205,461	202,727	+16.5%
+/- previous	+2.8%	+7.5%	+9.3%	-1.3%	

(*Excludes subscriptions to electronic journals)

Source: SCONUL Annual Library Statistics 2007-2008, Society of College, National & University Libraries (SCONUL) 2009

It should be noted that although 'electronic items' in the above table does not include electronic journals, it should not therefore be assumed that this entry refers exclusively to e-books. It also includes electronic data sets and so-called 'middleware' products (software programmes to enable federated searching, etc.). However, it can safely be stated that expenditure on e-books forms a substantial amount of the sums given, and that growing expenditure on e-books is responsible for much of the rapid year-on-year increases in the electronic items category. In the four-year period captured by these figures, expenditure on electronic items has increased by almost 41 per cent, whereas total expenditure has increased by only 16.5 per cent.

As in the US, the most efficient way for publishers to approach academic libraries is through their consortia. There are five consortia operating in England, and one each in Scotland and Wales. The five English consortia have recently combined to create a single 'super consortium' which in 2009 for the first time arranged contracts with certain suppliers on behalf

Figure 2.1   University library expenditure on electronic resources (excluding serials) 2006/07and 2007/08

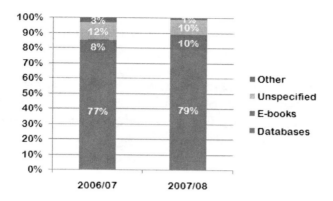

Source: SCONUL Annual Library Statistics 2007-2008, SCONUL 2009

NB: The number of universities providing breakdowns does vary between the years and between the different resources (see below).   Therefore unspecified is the difference between the total expenditure on electronic resources and the actual totals reported for databases, e-books and other.

Number of respondents on electronic resources	Total	Database	E-books	Other
Respondents 2007/08	133	119	115	99
Respondents 2006/07	131	117	112	99

of all of them. Most HEI libraries also deal with some publishers and aggregators on an individual basis. A further opportunitiy is offered by academics with research grants, which can be substantial, particularly when a group of academics is working together. Often these academics, whether working singly or in groups, prefer to purchase or license their own online materials independently of the library. (This often infuriates librarians, but that is not a problem for publishers!) Discovering these opportunities may take a little effort, but the rewards can be considerable.

2.3.4   Australia

Government

The Australian goverment launched its digital strategy - *Digital Economy: Future Directions* in July 2009[210].

The plan outlines the development and use of the national broadband network. It encourages the use of digital solutions for schools, health including social participation as well as summarises the government initiatives which will assist in this process.

Retail

The Australian Bureau of Statistics last published a report on publishing in 2005. Sales of electronic books (into which figure was incorporated sales of audiobooks – the two components are not broken down) then totalled A$7.5m, of which it can be safely assumed that audiobooks constituted the major share. Some Australian booksellers now sell e-books from their websites: for example, Dymocks[211]. Online retailers of e-books include Collins[212] and ebooks.com. There is as yet no Amazon Australia, but Australians also buy e-books from Amazon.com and Barnes & Noble. The Australian retail e-book market is hampered by the fact that few handheld readers are currently offered for sale there, though there is a great deal of consumer interest in e-books[213] which is waiting to be exploited more fully.

Schools

Australia generally, and the State of Victoria in particular, has been in the forefront of incorporating I.T. into schools and encouraging the use of online materials. In its 2008 Budget, the government committed AUS$2.2 billion over six years to its Digital Education Revolution initiative which included:

---

210 www.dbcde.gov.au/digital_economy/future_directions_of_the_digital_economy/australias_
     digital_economy_future_directions
211 www.dymocks.com.au/VirtualStore/landingPage.aspx?Store=Digital&Ne=10&N=4294967265
212 www.collinsbooks.com.au
213 See for example www.e-book.com.au/news.htm

- the allocation of AUS$100m for the further development of affordable, fast broadband services for school education
- AUS $32.6m to support the development and effective integration of digital learning resources and technical infrastructure in teaching and learning
- Aus $20m (of AUS$40m) for provision of support for professional development of teachers' ICT capability and leadership
- other support mechanisms to support the deployment of ICT in schools.

In May 2010, a further AUS$ 200m was provisionally allocated in the government's budget for 2013-24.

In 2001, the Copyright and Digital Agenda Bill required schools and other educational institutions to negotiate a licence for permission to copy parts of works, whether printed or produced by electronic or digital methods. The Australian Publisher's Association (APA) is active in working to raise the profile of educational publishers with the various governments and education departments, and also keen to prosecute illegal copying.

EDNA is a website for Australian educators at all levels which includes sections on using digital technology and publications[214].

Public libraries

Public libraries in Australia, like the ones in Canada, are organised and run by the individual states and territories. It is therefore necessary to carry out research into provision by each state in order to arrive at an overall analysis of opportunities for selling digital products. The quality of statistical analysis varies from state to state, but is on the whole quite comprehensive. Reports for most of the library services can be found at www.nla.gov.au.

---

214 www.edna.edu.au/edna/go/ict

Academic libraries in Australia and New Zealand

As with the USA and Canada, statistics for the HEI library market in Australia and New Zealand are combined, mainly because they have been collected by the Council of Australian University Libraries (CAUL) and the Council of New Zealand University Libraries (CONZUL) jointly. The full data set for 2008, published in 2009, can be viewed at www.caul.edu.au/stats/caul. The CAUL figures cover many different areas of educational expenditure (more, in fact than the ARL ones), and are published as Excel spreadsheets, not as tables, so it is not possible to include the relevant sections in their entirety in Table 2.4: only the ones relating to e-resources have been included. Unlike the ARL figures, they relate to all higher educational institutional organisatiions in the countries concerned.

Table 2.4: Electronic book sales in HEI libraries in Australia and New Zealand 2005-2007 (AUS $)

E-resources	2005	2006	2007	2008
Australia	$86,938,355	$102,356,415	$121,368,085	$145,291,288
+/- previous		+17%	+18%	+16.2%
New Zealand	$24,764,655	$26,644,732	$33,422,565	$38,836,828
+/- previous		+7.5%	+25%	+16.2%

Source: Council of Australian Universities Librarians (CAUL), http://www.caul.edu.au

It should be noted that the term 'e-resources' does not include electronic journals, but also does not relate solely to e-books. It includes datasets, database products and 'middleware'. Nevertheless, a large chunk of it will have been spent on e-books. The year on year percentage increases are also encouraging.

A list of Australia's universities can be found at: http://offshorewave.com/universities_listed_by_Country/Universities_in_Australia.html.

2.3.5   New Zealand

Government

New Zealand has a Digital Content Strategy, in the implementation of which both the national library and public libraries are heavily involved. It is part of the National Digital Strategy[215]. The Digital Content Strategy is explained as follows:

> *"Creating a Digital New Zealand is about making New Zealand visible and relevant in a connected digital world. It aims to ensure that we are innovative, informed and capable in telling our stories, experiencing our heritage and cultures, and creating our digital future. To that end, an important starting point for the strategy is recognising that the value of content is in what it delivers and enables for end-users. The strategy presents the key digital content influences in New Zealand's environment, an analysis of digital content issues, and the digital content challenges that face us as a nation. The first steps towards creating a digital New Zealand are outlined in a series of government actions, while related actions from other strategies that contribute directly to the outcomes of this strategy are identified."*

Helping New Zealand to fulfil the aims of the strategy appears to offer opportunities for both publishers and platform providers or conversion companies.

Retail

There are few digital initiatives taking place in book retailing in New Zealand, and little real likelihood of that changing in the near to medium term. The main retailers are the RED Group, which owns Whitcoulls (a WHS-like chain), and Borders. Both appear to be struggling to maintain their position in the marketplace in traditional print sales, and seem therefore to be preoccupied with other things besides going digital (although Whitcoulls does have an e-commerce site[216]). There is always the possibility that another, more unconventional, business may enter this

---

215 For a PDF of the full document, see www.digitalstrategy.govt.nz/Resources/New-Zealand-Digital-Content-Strategy/
216 www.arw.co.nz/arw_online_about_us.htm

space, but there is little evidence of that happening yet. No-one (except Amazon) has really space, grabbed the entrepreneurial retail possibilities of digital technology in New Zealand and made it simple for the end-user - for example, purchasers have to jump through many hoops to get an e-book version of Dan Brown from Random House - and user friendly.

Schools

On the educational front a much more encouraging picture exists. Digital offerings are more established, and the New Zealand school system is very forward thinking. Despite the fact that it is a government department, the National Library is an innovative and active player in the digital space and has literacy as one of its prime objectives. The various resources that it offers for schools appear on its website[217]. There are clearly opportunities for publishers to tap into here.

Learning Media[218] is a state owned enterprise (a lot of infrastructural organisations are owned by the government in New Zealand because the market is relatively small). It specialises in school books and learning resources. It is very active and has a big export market. Partnership with Learning Media, to exploit co-publishing opportunities, is an excellent way for publishers to make an impact on the New Zealand educational market.

Public libraries

The public library service in New Zealand is run by three bodies: Local government New Zealand, LIANZA[219], and the National Library of New Zealand. LIANZA has launched an initiative similar to the Public Library Standards issued by the UK government in 2001, which involves, among other things, plans for comprehensive ICT development in New Zealand's libraries; and that there is already in existence an 'Internet public library' there: see www.ipl.org.

217 www.natlib.govt.nz/schools
218 www.learningmedia.co.nz
219 www.lianza.org.nz

Public libraries in New Zealand are perhaps less embattled than their UK counterparts and, while currently under some financial pressure, are better resourced and in some ways technologically more advanced than UK public libraries. This is partly because they are more widely used than libraries in the UK for reading and borrowing books, rather than for other services, which in turn is because the flaws in the supply chain of books to New Zealand means that patrons are more likely to find non-bestseller titles at the library than in a bookshop. Libraries are also very interested in electronic lending. Information about most of the libraries in New Zealand, the types of service they offer and products that they are interested in may be found at:

http://webdirectory.natlib.govt.nz/dir/en/nz/general-and-reference/libraries/.

Academic libraries

(See also Australian section for CAUL statistics.)

The main library purchasing consortium set up exclusively for New Zealand is the Library Consortium of New Zealand (LCoNZ[220]). As well as uniting to purchase materials from both publishers and aggregators, it has enabled its members to digitise many of the processes connected with library administration, often basing their innovations on what is happening in libraries in the US[221]. As elsewhere in the world, an increasing proportion of the budgets of New Zealand's academic libraries is being committed to electronic resources.

A list of New Zealand's universities can be found at:
http://offshorewave.com/universities_listed_by_Country/Universities_in_New_Zealand.html

---

220 www.lconz.ac.nz
221 See, for example, www.lconz.ac.nz/news.html

2.3.6   Germany

Government

Germany's Federal government presented its national strategy for the development of broadband infrastructure in February 2009[222]. The strategy has two phases: connecting all households to broadband Internet by end-2010, and bringing 75% of the households under the coverage of 50 Mbps broadband by 2014.

Retail

The GfK (Gesellschaft für Konsumforschung), a market research and consumer insight agency, announced that 65,000 e-books were sold in Germany in the first half of 2009. This is a fairly impressive figure, given that virtually none of the best-known hand-held readers is currently available in Germany. However, at least two of the four big German wholesalers are in the process of setting up e-book platforms that will serve both their bookseller and their publisher clients, which, coupled with the imminent opening-up of e-reader accessibility, means that there will probably be significant growth in the German e-book market over the next year.

Libreka![223]

At the Frankfurt Book Fair 2007, a group of German publishers launched Libreka!, an Internet book search engine intended to rival Google. Libreka! is operated by MVB, a multi-service organisation which also produces *German Books in Print* and acts as the Book Industry Standards Agency for Germany. It has more than 128,000 works on offer and offers 24,000 ebooks in PDF and epub formats.

Unregistered users can go to the libreka! website enter a search word and are shown the titles of German books which contain that word, including images of the front covers, but not the contents.

---

222   www.broadband-europe.eu/Lists/StrategiesData/Attachments/25/Germany%20
      Broadband%20Strategy_EN.pdf
223   www.libreka.de

Libraries

In December 2009 the Federal government agreed to finance the development of a German Digital Library (Deutsche Digitale Bibliothek)[224]. The plan is to save digital copies of over 30,000 works from German cultural and scientific organisations to this library, which is expected to go live in 2011. The project will seek copyright holder's approval before making digital copies.

A list of libraries (public and HE) in Germany and Central Europe may be found at http://lists.webjunction.org/libweb/central.html.

Higher Education Institutions

A list of Germany's HEIs may be found at www.offshorewave.com/universities_listed_by_Country/Universities_in_Germany.html.

2.3.7   The Netherlands

The Netherlands has one of the highest broadband penetration according to the OECD[225], with 100 per cent capable of capable of receiving broadband service. This is due to large-scale government and municipal investment in broadband infrastructure.

Retail

Centraal Boekhuis[226], the largest Dutch wholesaler, launched an e-book platform in 2009. According to the Dutch Publishers Association, in the final quarter of 2009, the e-reader gained momentum although the number of ebook titles available and sold was still quite small. Up until June 2010, 37,000 e-readers were sold holding three titles average. The estimated number of e-book copies sold was 110,000.

---

224 www.deutsche-digitale-bibliothek.de
225 OECD Broadband statistics 2010
226 www.centraal.boekhuis.nl

Schools

In December 2008 the Dutch Ministry of Education announced the Wikiwijs project[227], an open, Internet-based platform, where teachers can find, download, (further) develop and share educational resources. The programme, developed by Open Universiteit Nederland[228] and Kennisnet[229] consists of five components:

- Access (an adequate technical infrastructure)

- Content (sufficient supply of educational resources)

- Communities (enthusiastic teachers having sufficient possibilities to connect to one another)

- Proficiency (proficient users who possess the knowledge and skill to deal with developing, arranging and/or using open, digital educational resources)

- Research (well-founded understanding of the results established by Wikiwijs)

The Wikiwijs platform was launched on 15 December 2009. Up until the start of school year 2010/2011, the project will remain in the trial phase and during this period only a few subjects will be covered i.e. Maths and Dutch language. More will be added when the platform is completed. Wikiwijs is scheduled to be fully operational at the start of the school year 2010/11. The scope of Wikiwijs is the whole Dutch educational system: from primary schools up to the universities.

Libraries

Koninklijke Bibliotheek[230], the National Library of the Netherlands, was the first national library in the world to have an operational digital deposit

---

227 http://wikiwijsinhetonderwijs.nl
228 www.ou.nl
229 www.kennisnet.nl
230 www.kb.nl

system based on the OAIS model. Built by IBM in close cooperation with KB, it became operational in March 2003.

In July 2010, KB and Google, signed an agreement under which Google will digitise more than 160.000 out-of-copyright (public domain) books from the library's collection. The books will be fully searchable and accessible for free via Google Books, via the various KB websites and - at a later date - via the European Union's Europeana portal.

Academic libraries

The 13 university libraries of the Netherlands together form a consortium which collates and analyses benchmarking information on library expenditure and use of resources. This information is not published; I am grateful to Henk Voorbij for allowing me to quote relevant extracts in Table 2.5.

Table 2.5: Summary of benchmarking survey of Dutch university libraries 2007

Collection expenditures €'000	Number of universities supplying data	Mean	Median	Minimum	Maximum
Printed and electronic books	13	548	490	155	1,080
Total journals	13	2,532	2651	936	4,125
Current printed journals	12	462	419	120	1,004
Electronic journals	12	1,925	1,689	556	3,482
Total print	12	911	747	367	2,084
Total electronic	11	2,283	1,984	1,091	4,502

Source: Henry Voorbij, National Library KB/Unmiversity of Amsterdam UvA

It can be seen from this table that the mean figure for expenditure on electronic resources other than journals by each of the Dutch universities was 358,000 euros in 2007; the median figure was 295,000 euros; the minimum figure (taking 'minimum' as total expenditure) was 535,000 euros; and the maximum figure (again taking 'maximum' as total expenditure) was 1,020,000 euros. (Note: obviously these figures are only approximate, because of the slightly varying numbers of submissions of various data received.) It will be noted that the universities with respectively the highest and the lowest budgets each spend more on electronic resources than the ones in the middle of the spectrum. It should be assumed that, as in the UK, non-journal electronic resources encompass a range of products, not just e-books.

2.3.8 Scandinavia

The *Global Information Technology Report 2009 – 2010,* published in March 2010 by the World Economic Forum, is the ninth in a series of such reports which offer a snapshot picture of the state of ICT network readiness in the countries of the world for the year in question. Under the general theme of 'ICT for sustainability', the report explores the central role of ICT in fostering economic, environmental and social sustainability, both as an industry in itself and in the overal economy and society. It covers 133 economies from the developing and developed world, representing more than 98% of global GDP, and rates their ICT performance on a broad range of factors.

In every year since the report was first produced, the Nordic countries have featured prominently. In 2009, Sweden was ranked first, Denmark third, Finland sixth, Norway tenth and Iceland twelfth. (for comparison, the USA was ranked fifth and the UK thirteenth). In the nine years that the report has appeared, a Nordic nation has topped the rankings on five occasions.

Sweden was runner-up in 2006, 2007 and 2008, and in 2009 overtook Denmark for the first time as the world's most ICT-developed economy. It scored 1st, 4th and 3rd for environment, readiness and usage respectively. The reports says: "Sweden displays the best and second-best infrastructure and regulatory environments in the world,with comprehensive and efficient hard infrastructure, top-class human resources and education infrastructure, and an extremely friendly regulatory framework ensuring full protection of intellectual property (second) and providing for comprehensive ICT laws (fourth). The market environment is also assessed as being very ICT-friendly at fifth place, notwithstanding very high taxation levels with a perceived distortive impact (111th for the extent and effect of taxation and 102nd for total tax rates."Sweden's excellent education system and its use of ICT for research and teaching is singled out for special mention in the report, which continues "(Education and Research) provides the ideal context for extensive ICT usage, especially by citizens (the report means 'ordinary people') (1st for individual usage), with among the highest penetration rates in the world for PCs (4th) and Internet and broadband Internet (both 2nd), as well as mobile telephony (29th, with 118.3 subscriptions per 100 population). The extremely sophisticated and innovative Swedish business sector is also benefitting fully from ICT in its activities and operations, ranking 1st in the world for the extent of business Internet usage."

The report's section on Denmark is quoted in full:

> "Denmark ranks 2nd for the quality of its environment and (ICT) readiness, but scores lower in terms of ICT usage (11th). The country features among the top 10 in all the pillars (attributes assessed) except one (17th in business usage). The conducive environment, coupled with an effective ICT vision and prioritisation by the government (5th and 8th in government readiness and usage, respectively), provide a unique basis for ICT development and innovation. Denmark continues to display among the highest ICT penetration rates in the world (4th for individual usage), with notably widespread Internet (4th) and broadband Internet (3rd) usage. Other notable competitive advantages are to be found in more general aspects, such as the well-functioning and developed internal market, which provided the national high-tech industry with a large domestic demand in its early stage; the top-notch education and research system(6th for the quality of the education system); and the taste and talent ofDanish citizens and businesses for developing, pioneering and using new technologies and applications."

Libraries

In Norway a digital library framework project was set up through the Norwegian Digital Library Initiative, a five year national programme started in 2003 by the newly formed Norwegian Archive, Library and Museum Authority to integrate digital resources and services on the Internet. Originally encompassing all types of libraries as well as archives and museums, the initiative was redefined in 2007 to focus on the challenges of the library sector. Implementation has been hindered by a lack of central government funding.

The National Library of Norway in its strategy documents from 2005, defined its main goal to be to 'form the core of the Norwegian Digital Library" and by Spring of 2009, the digital collection included 90,000 books and 200,000 newspapers, compared to none in 2005. On 23 April 2009 the National Library signed a contract with Kopinor, the Norwegian RRO, regarding a pilot project called Bokhylla.no ('Bookshelf') for digital books on the Internet. Through this project, the National Library will makes accessible in full text digitised works from the 1690s, the 1790s the 1890s and the 1990s to Norwegian IP-addresses. Bokhylla.no, which is a service of Nbdigital,[231], was launched in May 2009, with 10,000 books under copyright and it is expected to reach 50,000 by the end of 2010. It is a three-year project due for evaluation in 2011. For further information on this project and the agreement with Kopinor, visit Kopinor's website at: www.kopinor.no.

The RROs in Sweden and Denmark are Bonus Presskopia (www.b-pk.se) and Copy-Dan (www.copydan.dk) respectively. It should be noted that all three of the RROs are interested in the legitimate digitisation and sale of publications online and are members of IFFRO.

In Denmark, the digital strategy revolved around the creation of an electronic research library only. The Denmark Denmark's Electronic Research Library (DEFF)[232] was launched as a five year project in 1997 co-financed by the Ministry of Science, Technology and Innovation, the Ministry of Culture and the Ministry of Education. However, by the end of

---

231 http://nbdigital.no
232 www.deff.dk

2002, the ministries decided to make it a permanent organisation with its own funding on the national budget. Since 2003 DEFF has functioned as an organisational collaboration between education and research libraries in Denmark with an annual budget of 2.3m euros and the secretariat is run by The Danish Agency for Libraries and Media. DEFF activities are focused on:

- E-Learning
- E-publishing
- Licenses
- Portals
- System architecture
- User facilities

In 2007, DEFF submitted a strategy discussion paper[233] on the role of and issues for digital libraries.

In Sweden, the Royal Library in Stockholm and representatives of the Swedish Writers Union (SFF), Swedish Publishers Association (SVF) signed an agreement in December 2009 to digitilise older works (which cannot be bought in printed form or as en e-book) and make them available on the library's website. The SFF and SVF will cooperate with rights holders and producers over copyright, while KB will be responsible for setting up the portal. It will start with a pilot project on the theme of the 1940s.

The Swedish government held a consultation between February and April 2010 requesting submissions on a national digital strategy, electronic access and preservation including costings. The Royal Library and approximately 50 institutions have submitted papers[234].

233 www.deff.dk/content.aspx?itemguid={C017EFBD-93EC-4815-9777-E3B79B8CDFA2}
234 www.kb.se/english/about/news/Digital-task/

Schools

During the last 10-20 years Danish governments have formed a number of ICT policies in education and have focused on:

- Infrastructure
- Development of learning resources
- Integration of ICT in subject matters
- ICT education for teachers (and pupils)

In 1999, the Danish Ministry of Education launched a national portal (EMU)[235] for learning resources for school, colleges and adult education. It hosts a number of sub websites including: The Subject Matter Info guide, the E-museum, SkoDA, and the National Repository of Learning Resources. Most of these services are free of charge.

In Norway, there have been two initiatives to provide digital textbooks for Norwegian students and teachers:

- **National Digital Learning Area (NDLA)**[236]. is a joint initiative of 18 of the 19 counties in Norway (except the City of Oslo), funded by the Ministry of Education. NDLA started in 2007 with the following guidelines from the Ministry of Education:

  - To increase access to and use of digital teaching aids in secondary education
  - Developing secondary schools and school owner's competence to order and/or develop digital learning resources
  - To increase the volume and diversity of digital educational materials aimed at secondary schools
  - Over time, reduce students' expenses for teaching aids

235 www.emu.dk
236 http://ndla.no

- Diglib[237] is a co-operation between Its Learning, leading learning platform provider to the education sector in Norway, and a number of publishers of digital content including Cappelen, NS Damm, Golden and Aschehoug, and Grieg Music Education. It is aimed at simplifying the distribution of digital content to the schools and higher education sector.

Sweden has a national education portal[238] – developed in 1994 by the Ministry of Education and run by the Swedish Agency for School Improvement. It provides links to digital learning resources, courses in the use of ICT and computer programmes. Its most popular services are:

- Lexin: A virtual dictionary

- Link Library (Länskafferiet): a search-and-retrieve service developed for use in the day-to-day work of schools. It is intended primarily for pupils between the ages of 10 and 15 and as such contains only material that has been examined for quality

- the Multimedia Bureau, which offers resources for publishing on the Internet.

Higher education

A list of Norway's universities can be found at:
http://offshorewave.com/universities_listed_by_Country/Universities_in_Norway.html

A list of Sweden's universities can be found at:
http://offshorewave.com/universities_listed_by_Country/Universities_in_Sweden.html

A list of Denmark's universities can be found at:
http://offshorewave.com/universities_listed_by_Country/Universities_in_Denmark.html

---

237 www.diglib.no
238 www.skolverket.se/sb/d/2366

2.3.9   France

Government

France has a national digital strategy, *The Development Plan for the Digital Economy by 2012*[239]. was unveiled in October 2008 by the Secretary of State to the Prime Minister, with responsibility for Forward Planning, the Assessment of Public Policies and the Development of the Digital Economy. Its four core priorities are:

- To enable all citizens to access all digital networks and services;

- To develop the production and supply of digital contents;

- To increase and diversify the use of digital services by companies, public administrations and citizens;

- To modernise the governance of the digital economy.

Retail

The main Internet booksellers are Alpapage, FNAC and Amazon. Hachette owns Virgin, Le Furet du Nord and Relay.   Numilog is the main e-book aggregator in France. French institutions and companies invest heavily in the online subscription services offered by professional, scientific and legal publishers. The Syndicat National de l'Edition estimates that total sales of e-books represented less than 1 per cent of total book sales (which were 2.85bn euros) in 2008. All the difficulties about recording reliable sales data for electronic publications already mentioned also apply to France.

France's largest publishers[240] announced in May 2010 that they would launch a joint e-book distribution platform by mid-June 2010, with the

---

239 http://lesrapports.ladocumentationfrancaise.fr/BRP/084000664/0000.pdf
240 The publishers involved in the venture include Eden Books (Flammarion, Gallimard, La Martinière/Le Seuil); Eplateforme (Editis, Média Participations, Michelin) and Numilog (owned by the Hachette Book Group).

system expected to be fully operational by September 2010. The launch took place on 25 June 2010 [241].

Public libraries

The French public library system is sophisticated. Of the 2,795 municipal libraries (2003 figures), 1,479 had a room dedicated to listening to/lending audio material and 841 had a video library. Most now offer online access to patrons.

A list of French libraries interested in acquiring digital products may be found at: http://lists.webjunction.org/libweb/France.html.

Schools

The Ministry of Education has been pursuing an active policy for encouraging online learning since 1998 – the *Action Plan for the Information Society* (PAGSI [242]). This has been successful in incorporating ICT into all teaching programmes at all levels, and is responsible for the proliferation of sophisticated educational websites and the involvement of the relevant educational bodies in setting up digital campuses. The initiative has made France an international leader in the use of ICT at primary, secondary and vocational levels. Renater[243], the research and education network, education network, supports high-speed technology to enable growth in the ICT infrastructure. Education authorities thus have the resources required to respond to the growing needs of schools by joining regional networks alongside other public users of Renater. Internet access systems using digital satellite and terrestrial links are also used. Each education authority has an adviser for ICT (a CTICE), who has a team of experts to implement ICT in education policy. 8,000 technological assistants in schools ensure that ICT resources are used properly. French teachers prefer to use supplementary learning materials, including online ones, to straightforward course books.

---

241 http://blog.epagine.fr/index.php/2010/06/loffre-commune-deden-livres-epagine-eplateforme-et-numilog-1ere-phase
242 www.education.gouv.fr/realisations/communication/samra.htm.
243 www.renater.fr

Télélangue[244] and Aurolag[245] are examples of companies that adopt an e-learning approach to language teaching. Pearson and OUP both offer online business courses in France.

700,000 people in France follow distance-learning courses each year, two-thirds of whom are adults and half of whom are pursuing a higher education qualification. Most are studying courses arranged by the National Centre for Distance Learning (NCED), which maintains a Campus Electronique for online access to courses and tuition. Some individual universities in France also offer distance learning.

Masson and Elsevier have led in the development of special Medical publishing websites. The majority of French legal publishing is delivered online. Market leaders are Elsevier; Lefebvre; Wolters Kluwer; (Editions Législatives; Vivendi and Revue Fiduciaire. Business and Management books – often with accompanying online support materials – sell well. These are most frequently translations of American titles.

A list of French universities may be found at:
www.offshorewave.com/country_profile_show.php?country_
id=71&directory_group_id=1

2.3.10 Spain

The following is a general commentary, as there is not enough information available (and possibly not enough activity at present) to provide information under different sector headings.

In Spain, the e-book market is in its infancy, but developing fast. There are as yet no models for supply, except in a few niche markets, e.g., for legal and reference works. In 2007, around 10.5 per cent of the total gross income of the publishing sector in Spain came from non-paper publications. Out of this, 70 per cent came from DVDs and CD-ROMs, and 10 per cent from online products: this is about one per cent of total gross publishing income. (Roughly similar to the UK at the beginning of this decade.)

244 www.telelangue.com
245 www.tellmemore.com

There are some specific e-business models run by entities like the collecting societies. CEDRO[246], the copyright collective management organisation (the Spanish equivalent to the UK's CLA and the US's CCC), deals with the collective licensing of certain digital uses of text works,whether they were originally in hard copy or 'digital born'. In many kinds of organisation – e.g., HEIs, private companies, public offices, etc. – it is common practice to make available to members or users excerpts of text works (either parts of printed works which are digitised for this purpose or digital born works). Therefore, there is a 'latent market' in Spain. It has yet to be fully exploited by the publishers, but the underlying culture needed for a receptive audience has already been created.

CEDROS's licences authorise use within the framework of the Spanish legislation on copyright. Such licences are granted based on specific mandates given to CEDRO by authors and publishers who are members of the organisation, as well as through the mandate of rightsholders represented by foreign RROs with which CEDRO has bilateral relations. There are no figures available about the size of this market in Spain. CEDRO has granted 27 licences so far, some to big organisations such as universities (but comparison with the UK's CLA, which has granted many thousands of licences, indicates that this is still a developing market).

In the retail sector, downloads of digital books are increasing rapidly. BUBOK[247] (a digital bookstore at the moment focused mainly on self-publishing), says that downloads have increased fourfold over the past year. Since portable e-readers have now arrived in Spain, this trend will probably accelerate quite fast. Some publishers and e-distributors have started to sell single e-books. STM and religious publishers are the pioneers.

There are two main organisations in Spain that deal with facilitating book content search on the Internet. DILVE[248] is a repository of books-in-print information, managed by the Spanish Publishers Association (FGEE). It contains rich metadata (ONIX-based) about books in-print and its main objective is to provide useful market-ready information to the book supply chain, rather than being a platform for searching book content. Perhaps

246 www.cedro.org/ingles_inicio.asp
247 www.bubok.com
248 www.dilve.es/dilve/dilveweb/index_dilve.jsp

even more important from an e-book perspective is the public-private partnership (called ODIBNE-Pro) between the Spanish National Library (BNE) and the FGEE. The ODIBNE-Pro[249] (Protected Digital Offer in the Spanish National Library) is a joint initiative whose objective is to set up a centre for the 'analysis, definition, development and dissemination of models of integration and exploitation of copyrighted digital contents in digital library environments'.

The idea stems from recognition that there is the lack of a model to establish the terms under which such a service could be provided, which prevents libraries from offering some form of access to copyrighted works. In its first phase, the project's pilot objective will be to integrate copyrighted digital works in the Spanish Digital Library (BDH), which was inaugurated in January 2008 by the BNE. It will act as a guide for the future actions of the centre and a test bed for future progress.

The chosen model is that the BDH will have at its disposal the necessary information to allow its users to perform a full text search of copyrighted books and to access complete bibliographic data (supplied by the publishers) and additional features such as cover images, summaries, indexes and samples of the works' content. From search results in the BDH, users will have the opportunity to be redirected to an e-distribution platform (an aggregator's/distributor's site), in order to further browse the book, have access to full text, download the book, etc., according to the specific business models and commercial conditions established by publishers. Works in the public domain will be accessible free of charge directly from the BDH website. It is therefore a joint public/private sector initiative which will provide publishers with a ready distribution channel for e-content.

The BNE has established some criteria for the selection of copyright works to be included in the project: priority of text over images, preference for original works over critical ones and priority for works strictly related to culture (so not school books, comics, manuals, etc.). Publishers providing e-books will have to prove their ownership of the corresponding digital rights. Only digital versions of existing printed works will be considered; full text display or download will be provided under the technical and

---

249 http://es-es.facebook.com/note.php?note_id=50384258368

commercial conditions established by the publishers. Publishers will keep e-distribution platforms operative for the duration of the project (which may be indefinite if it is successful) and will provide the necessary accompanying metadata. They will have to provide the following: a file with the full text of the work, for indexation purposes (in PDF format); the additional information that will be presented about the work (cover, summary, etc.); a sample of the work for displaying (again in PDF; it is recommended it contains the index and a significant excerpt of the book, possibly around 20 per cent). They will also make each e-book file available in the e-distribution platform of their choice, according to the commercial conditions established by them.

Publishers will select the books they intend to make available to the project, and will sign the subsequent agreements with the BNE and FGEE. They will then produce the necessary files, metadata and rich catalogue data. DILVE, the Spanish Internet platform that manages bibliographic and commercial information for book sector professionals, will take charge of handling the metadata.

The aim of ODIBNE-Pro is to digitise and incorporate in the BDH some 2,000 copyrighted books; these will complement the BNE's digital collection of some 10,000 public domain works which have been available to users since the beginning of 2008. At the end of 2008, the BNE undertook a massive digitisation programme, sponsored by the telecom company Telefónica, which should result in the addition of some 200,000 more works over the next five years.

The project has received subsidies from the Spanish Ministry of Industry, Tourism and Trade within the framework of the Avanza Content Sub-programme, part of a broader government initiative aimed at fostering innovation and the adoption of information technologies by enterprises. Part of the subsidy will be given to publishers to cover the costs of digitisation. This is the first type of public support to have been made available in Spain for the digitisation of books by publishers; there are no specific policies relating to it; it seems rather to be in the nature of an experiment.

ODIBNE-Pro started at the end of 2008 and it is currently in a preparatory and study stage (technical needs, selection of publishers, etc.); it should become operational after summer 2009, with a pilot project involving 45 works. It is an important project, and will act as a major catalyst for the adoption of e-books by Spain.

Besides the ODIBNE-Pro there are a few other small initiatives - trade projects that are being conducted as experiments between publishers and booksellers.

As well as the BDH, other institutions have digitised many works in the public domain. The private University of Alicante, sponsored by the Santander Bank, is running the Biblioteca Virtual Cervantes, which allows access to works in the public domain and envisages that it will soon include works under copyright, which will mean guaranteeing fair remuneration to rightsholders through specific separate agreements. BUBOK, as a digital bookstore, is dealing with some public libraries at the national level, and helping the digitisation and the dissemination of their collections.

A consortium led by the three largest publishers in Spain has recently set up an e-book platform - Libranda [250]. Several smaller publishers are also placing e-books on this platform.

A list of universities in Spain can be found at:
http://offshorewave.com/universities_listed_by_Country/Universities_in_ Spain.html.

---

[250] www.libranda.com

Afterword

This report seeks to address most of the areas with which publishers need to be concerned when they are 'going digital', either for the first time or because they are seeking to extend their existing digital offer. It has attempted to be up-to-date while treating untried, very new concepts with caution, and to provide enough information to enable those reading it to take specific items of interest further, but without covering in detail basic issues with which most publishers are already conversant.

Bearing these points in mind, the report is inevitably not entirely comprehensive – otherwise it would be many more pages longer than it is – and necessarily quite light on statistics, because the digital sector in general, and the trade organisations which serve the publishing industry in particular, have only recently made (still tentative) attempts to collate data on digital sales and expenditure. Furthermore, the countries that at present have made the most extensive attempts to capture such statistics are the Anglophone countries, especially the USA and the UK; but the report has set itself a wider international scope, which it is hoped will be extended still further in subsequent editions.

Many third parties with whom publishers can choose to partner, or from whom they can seek advice, have been described briefly, and their contact details given. It should, however, be emphasised that the list is by no means exhaustive, and that the omission of information about any particular company or organisation does not imply that its products and services are not endorsed. Future editions will add other potential partners as appropriate. Similarly, information given about possible purchasers of publishers' products, although it is already extensive in some areas (notably the HE library sector), will be augmented in future editions.

The report is designed primarily for publishers, and an attempt has been made to set it out in ways that will be of most practical use to them. However, it is hoped that it will also be of interest to all of the parties who form part of the electronic publishing creation and supply chain, including authors, librarians, retailers, digital service providers, trade organisations and public bodies, and academics and students interested in publishing, whether they live and work in the UK or elsewhere in the world

There are many people whom I ought to thank, but unfortunately they are too numerous to mention. They know who they are, and I hope that I have thanked all of them individually. A special mention should be made to Mandy Knight of the PA, for her conscientious support, patience and unfailing good humour; to Graham Taylor, for his incisive editing of the first draft and to Steve Schatz of LibreDigital, who has kindly turned it into an e-book.

Linda Bennett
August 2010

Part Three | References

3.1   List of the e-book readers in the retail market

Note: I am indebted to Sydney Davies, Trade Practices Executive of the Booksellers Association, for extensive help in keeping this list up-to-date

3.1.1   Most important e-book readers

iPad
Manufacturer: Apple Inc. (Foxconn)
Website: www.apple.com/ipad
Physical features: 242.8mm x189.7mmx13.4mm. Weight: Wi-Fi model: 680gms; Wi-Fi+3G model: 730gms. Multi-touch screen, headset controls, proximity and ambient light sensors, 3-axis accelerometer, magnetometer.
Document types: iBooks from App Store, various magazines.
Capacity: 16GB, 32GB or 64GB
Other Media: Safari, e-mail, photos, video, YouTube, iPod, iTunes, etc.

Kindle
Manufacturer: Amazon
Website: www.amazon.com
Physical features: Weight 10oz, 7.5in x 5.3in x 0.7in, 6in E-Ink display, 600 x 800 pixels on 4 level gray scale, QWERTY keyboard, 6 font sizes, audio, wireless Whispernet (EVDO)
Document types: Word, HTML, TXT, JPEG, GIF, BMP, PNG, PRC, MOBI
Titles: Holds 200+ titles, optional SD memory, eg 256MB = 300 (New Oxford American Dictionary included)
Titles available: 230,000
News & other media available: 40+ Newspapers/Magazines on subscription, 800+ blogs

Sony Reader PRS-505
Manufacturer: Sony
Website: www.sony.co.uk
Physical features: Weight 260g, 122mm x 175.3mm x 7.6mm, 6in E-Ink display, 170 pixels in 8 level grey scale, audio, USB to PC XP/Vista
Document types: EPUB, BBeB, PDF, Word, TXT, RTF, JPEG, GIF, PNG, BMP
Titles: Holds 160+ titles, optional DUO SD memory 13,000 titles (includes 100 free classics)
Titles available: 45,000 (Sony US) – 6,000 (Waterstone's).

Sony Reader PRS-700

Manufacturer: Sony

Website: www.sony.com

Physical features: Weight 10oz, 122mm x 175.3mm x 7.6mm, 6in E-Ink display, 170 pixels in 8 level grey scale, touch screen, LED reading light, audio, USB to PC XP/Vista

Document types: EPUB, BBeB, PDF, Word, TXT, RTF, JPEG, GIF, PNG, BMP

Titles: Holds 350+ titles

Titles available: 57,000 (Sony US)

News & other media available: N/A

enTourage eDGe(TM)

Manufacturer: Entourage

Website: www.entourageedge.com

Physical features: Weight: 3lbs, 8.25' x 10.75' x 1.0' (closed), LCD Touchscreen display size: 1024 x 600, e-paper display size: 9.7" e-Ink®(1200x825), 8 shades of grey, e-paper input: Wacom®;Penabled®. Input: stylus input on e-paper and touchscreen.

Document types: ePub, PDF

Titles: has 3 gigabytes of usable memory

Audio playback: MP3, WAV, 3GPP, MP$, AAC, OGG, M4A

Video playback: 3GP, MP4, Adobe Flashlight

BeBook

Manufacturer: Endless Ideas BV

Website: http://mybebook.com/

Physical features: Weight 220g, 184mm x 120mm x 10mm, 6in E-Ink display, audio, USB to PC & MAC

Document types: PDF, MOBI, LIT, EPUB, HTML, TXT, PRC, RTF, FB2, JPG, TIF

Titles: Holds 1,000+ titles, SD slot (includes 150 free titles)

Titles available: 80,000

News & other media available: 300,000 of free RSS newsfeeds

Cybook Gen3

Manufacturer: Bookeen

Website: www.bookeen.com

Physical features: Weight 6oz/175g, 118mm x 188mm x 8.5mm, 6in E-Ink display, 4 grayscale, 600 x 800 pixels, audio, USB to PC

Document types: HTML, TXT, PRC, PalmDoc, PDF, MOBI, JPEG, GIF, PNG

Titles: Holds 200+, SD slot for 1,000

Titles available: 55,000

News & other media available: RSS feeds

Nook

Proprietary e-reader of Barnes & Noble

Website: www.barnesandnoble.com/nook/index

Physical features: Weight 12.1ozs, 7.7 inches x4.9 inches x 0.5 inches, E-Ink®Vizplex electronic paper display

Document types: ePub, PDB, PDF, JPEG, GIF,PNG, BMP, MP3

Titles: 2GB (approx. 1500 e-books)

Titles available: from Barnes & Noble website only

jetBook

Manufacturer: ECTACO

Website: www.jetbook.net

Physical features: Weight 7.4oz/210g, 153mm x 109mm x 13mm, 5in TFT, grayscale, audio, USB to PC

Document types: TXT, PDF, FB2, JPG, GIF, PNG, BMP

Titles: Up to 1,000 (includes bilingual dictionaries)

Titles available: 500,000

News & other media available: N/A

Pixelar E-Reader

Manufacturer: Pixelar

Website: www.pixelar.co.uk

Physical features: Weight 7.4oz/210g, 184mm x 125mm x 10mm, 4 grayscale, 600 x 800 pixels, 1GB SD card, audio, USB to PC & MAC

Document types: TXT, PDF, FB2, JPG, GIF, PNG, BMP, MOBI, HTML, TIF, PPT, EPUB, LIT

Titles: Up to 1,000

Titles available: N/A

News & other media available: RSSUK

Readius

Manufacturer: Polymer Vision

Website: www.readius.com

Physical features: Weight 115g, 115mm x 57mm x 21mm, E-Ink 5in flexible rollable display, 16 grey levels, USB, Bluetooth

Document Types: HTML, PDF, ASCII, JPEG, PNG, GIF, BMP

Titles: N/A

Titles available: N/A

News & other media available: RSS feeds

3.1.2   Other e-readers

Alex

Manufacturer: Spring Design

Website: www.springdesign.com

Boox

Manufacturer: Onyx International

Website: www.onyx-international.com

Elonex eBook

Manufacturer: Elonex

Website: www.elonex.co.uk

EZ Reader

Manufacturer: Astak

Website: www.astak.com

FLEPia

Manufacturer: Fujitsu Frontech

Website: www.frontech.fujitsu.com

Foxit Reader
Manufacturer: Foxit
Website: www.foxitsoftware.com

Hanlin E-Reader
Manufacturer: Pixelar
Website: www.pixelar.co.uk

Hexaglot
Manufacturer: Hexaglot
Website: www.hexaglot.com

Libre
Manufacturer: Aluratek
Website: www.aluratek.com

MiBook
Manufacturer: Photocol Inc
Website: www.mibook.com

Netronix EB-500 & EB-600 & EB-610 & EB-611 & EB-900
Manufacturer: Netronix
Website: www.netronixinc.com

Mentor
Manufacturer: Astak
Website: www.astak.com

Palm Reader
Manufacturer: Palm Digital Media
Website: www.palm.com

Samsung
Manufacturer: Samsung
Website: www.samsung.com

Skiff
Manufacturer: Skiff
Website: www.skiff.com

Txtr Reader
Manufacturer: Wizpac
Website: www.txtr.com

3.1.3   E-Reader Software

Mobipocket Reader
Devices: Smartphone, Blackberry, PDA
Manufacturer: Mobipocket
Website: www.mobipocket.com

Fictionwise eReader
Devices: iPhone, iPod Touch
Manufacturer: Fictionwise
Website: www.fictionwise.com

Iceberg
Devices: iPhone, iPod Touch
Manufacturer: ScrollMotion
Website: www.scrollmotion.com
iReadingDevices: iPhone, iPod Touch
Manufacturer: Norbsoft
Website: http://en.norbsoft.com/

Stanza
Devices: iPhone, iPod Touch, Kindle
Manufacturer: Lexcycle
Website: www.lexcycle.com

GoSpoken
Devices: Audio for all mobiles
Manufacturer: GoSpoken
Website: www.gospoken.com

Others

Blio eReader: KNFB Reading Technology
www.blioreader.com

BookShelf: BookShelf
www.iphonebookshelf.com

The Bookstore App: Barnes & Noble
www.barnesandnoble.com

eReader: eReader
www.ereader.com

Eucalyptus: Things Made Out of Other
Things
www.eucalyptusapp.com

Google Mobile: Google
http://books.google.com

Iceberg: ScrollMotion
www.scrollmotion.com

iSilo: iSilo
www.isilo.com

Microsoft Reader: Microsoft
www.microsoft.com/Reader/

Plucker: Plucker
www.plkr.org

Wattpad: Wattpad
www.wattpad.com

3.2   Library consortia worldwide and international organisations interested in e-publications

Anatolia

Anatolian University Libraries
Consortium (ANKOS)
Izmir Institute of Technology
Gulbahce Koyu, 35430 Izmir
Turkey
Tel: +90 232 750 6330
Fax +90 232 750 6333
Email: baskan@ankos.gen.tr
www.ankosnet.org

Argentina

Base de Datos Unificada (BDU)
Consorcio SIU
Av. Santa Fe 1548 Piso 11 "Frente"
Argentina
Tel: +54 11 4129 1953
Fax: +54 11 4129 1953
Email: ipineiro@siu.edu.ar
http://bdu.siu.edu.ar
Executive Director: Lic. Luján Gurmendi
Email: lujan@siu.edu.ar

Biblioteca Electrónica de Ciencia y
Tecnología de la República Argentina
(BE - MINCYT)
Av. Córdoba 831, 7mo piso
(C1054AAH) Ciudad Autónoma de
Buenos Aires - Argentina
Tel: +54 11 4891 8300
Fax: +54 11 4891 8907
Email: info@biblioteca.mincyt.gov.ar
www.biblioteca.mincyt.gov.ar

Australia

Council of Australian University
Librarians (CAUL)
LPO Box 8169 (Licensed Post Office)
Australian National University
Canberra ACT 2601
Australia
Tel: +61 2 6125 2990
Fax: +61 2 6248 8571
www.caul.edu.au
Executive Director: Diane Costello
Email: diane.costello@caul.edu.au

CAVAL Co-operative Solutions
CAVAL Ltd
4 Park Drive
Bundoora, Victoria, 3083
Australia
Tel: +61 3 9459 2722
Fax: +61 3 9459 2733
Email: caval@caval.edu.au
www.caval.edu.au

Commonwealth Scientific and Industrial
Research Organisation (CSIRO)
Locked Bag 10
Clayton South VIC 3169
Australia
Tel: +61 3 9545 2176
Fax: +61 3 9545 2175
Email - Enquiries@csiro.au
www.csiro.au/

National and State Libraries of Australia
(NSLA Consortium)
Parkes Place
Canberra ACT 2600
Australia
Tel: +61 2 6262 1549
Fax: +61 2 6273 1180
Email: nslaconsortium@nla.gov.au
www.nslaconsortium.org.au

Gulliver Group
c/o Viclink Inc
P.O. Box 509
Mooroolbark VICTORIA 3138
Australia
Tel: +61 3 9725 2725
Fax +61 3 8625 0079
Email: jrae@chrlc.vic.gov.au
www.libraries.vic.gov.au/gulliver

Queensland University Libraries Office of Cooperation
Staffed by an Executive Officer on a part-time basis, the secretariat is generally located within the institution of the Convenor of QULOC. The convenorship rotates on a two year cycle
www.quloc.org.au

UNILINC Limited
Level 9, 210 Clarence Street
Sydney NSW 2000
Australia
Tel: +61 2 9283 1488
Fax: +61 2 9267 9247
Email: query@unilinc.edu.au
www.unilinc.edu.au

Austria

Kooperation E-Medien Österreich
(Austrian Academic Consortium: KEMOE/
AAC)
Die Österreichische Bibliothekenverbund
und Service GmbH
Brünnlbadgasse 17/2a
A-1090 Vienna
Austria
Tel: +43 1 403 5158-18
Fax: +43 1 403 5158-30
www.konsortien.at
Contact : helmut.hartmann
Email: helmut.hartmann@obvsg.at

Azerbaijan

Azerbaijan Library and Information Consortium (AZLIC)
ala B. Hajibayova
National Coordinator of eIFL.net project in
Azerbaijan
Tel: +99 450 352 3942
Email: AzLIC@aznet.org
www.azlic.aznet.org

Belgium

Bibliothèque interuniversitaire de la Communauté française de Belgique (BICfB)
c/o SCEB
Place de l'Université 1
1348 Louvain-la-Neuve
Belgique
Email: bicfb-sceb@listes.uclouvain.be
www.bicfb.be

Vlaams Overlegorgaan inzake
Wetenschappelijk Bibliotheekwerk
(Flemish Research Libraries Council)
(VOWB)
VOWB - Secretariat
Universiteitsbibliotheek
Mgr. Ladeuzeplein 21, PB 5591
B-3000 Leuven
Tel: +32 16 324 609
Fax +32 16 324 644
Cordinator: K. Van Wonterghem
Email: kaat.vanwonterghem@vowb.be
www.vowb.be/voorstelling_en.html

Botswana

Botswana Libraries Consortium
C/O University of Botswana Library
Private Bag 00390
Gaborone
Botswana
Tel: +267 355 2297
Fax: +267 395 7291
Email: mbaakany@mopipi.ub.bw

Brazil

Programa de Apoio a Aquisicao de
Periodicos -- PAAP (Portal.periodicos
CAPES)
Caixa Postal 365, Esplanada dos
Ministérios - Bloco "L" - Anexo II - sala
206, CEP.: 70.359-970 Brasília – DF
Brazil
Tel: +55 61 2104 8857
Fax: +55 61 2104 9631
Email: periodicos@capes.gov.br
www.periodicos.capes.gov.br

Canada

The Alberta Library (TAL)
6-14, 7 Sir Winston Churchill Square
Edmonton, Alberta T5J 2V5
Canada
Tel: +1 780 414 0805
Fax: +1 780 414 0806
www.thealbertalibrary.ab.ca

The Bibliocentre
31 Scarsdale Road.
North York, Ontario
Canada M3B-2R2
Tel: +1 647 722 9300
Fax: +1 647 722 9301
www.bibliocentre.ca

British Columbia Electronic Library
Network (BC ELN)
W.A.C. Bennett Library, 7th Floor
Simon Fraser University
8888 University Drive
Burnaby, BC V5A 1S6
Canada
Tel: +1 778 782 7003
Fax: +1 778 782 3023
Email: office@eln.bc.ca
www.eln.bc.ca

Canadian Research Knowledge Network
200 - 343 Preston Street
Preston Square, Tower II
Ottawa Ontario K1S 1N4
Canada
Tel: +1 613 907 7040
Fax: +1 866 903 9094
www.ResearchKnowledge.ca

Conférence des recteurs et des
principaux des universités du Québec
(CREPUQ)
500, rue Sherbrooke Ouest, bureau 200
Montréal H3A 3C6
Canada
Tel: +1 514 288 8524
Fax: +1 514 288 0554
Email : info@crepuq.qc.ca
www.crepuq.qc.ca

Consortium of Ontario Libraries (COOL)
Southern Ontario Library Service
111 Peter Street, Suite 902
Toronto, Ontario M5V 2H1
Canada
Tel: +1 416 961 1669 x 5104
Fax: +1 416 961 5122
Email: bfranchetto@sols.org
www.library.on.ca/ResourceSharing/
coolcpa/whatiscool.htm

Council of Atlantic University Libraries
(CAUL-CDBUA)
1550 Bedford Hwy, #501
Bedford, Nova Scotia B4A 1E6
Canada
Tel: +1 506 458 7053
Fax: +1 506 453 4595
www.caul-cdbua.ca
Coordinator of Digital Licensing: Jocelyne
Thompson
Email: jlt@unb.ca

Council of Federal Libraries Consortium
(CFLC) -- Conseil des bibliothèques du
gouvernement fédérale (CBGFC)
395 Wellington Street
Ottawa, Ontario K1A 0N4
Canada
Tel: +1 819 934 7427
Fax: +1 819 934 7534
Email: FLCS-SCBGF@lac-bac.gc.ca
www.collectionscanada.ca/consortium/
index-e.html

Council of Prairie and Pacific University
Libraries (COPPUL)
2005 Sooke Road
Victoria, British Columbia
Canada V9B 5Y2
Tel: +1 250 391 2554
Fax: +1 250 391 2556
Email: coppul@royalroads.ca
www.coppul.ca
Executive Director: Mr. Alexander Slade

Health Knowledge Network
1494 Health Sciences Centre
3330 Hospital Drive NW
Calgary, AB
T2N 4N1
Tel: + 1 403 220 8250
Fax: + 1 403 210 9847
Email: vstieda@ucalgary.ca
www.hkn.ca

Health Science Information Consortium
of Toronto (HSICT)
c/o Gerstein Science Information Centre
University of Toronto
9 King's College Circle
Toronto, Ontario M5S 1A5
Canada
Tel: +1 416 978 6359
Fax: +1 416 971 2637
www.library.utoronto.ca/hsict
Executive Director: Miriam Ticoll
Email: :miriam.ticoll@utoronto.ca

Manitoba Library Consortium Inc. (MLCI)
c/o Library Administration
University of Winnipeg
515 Portage Ave
Winnipeg MB R3B 2E9
Canada
Fax: +1 204 783 8910 (c/o MLCI)
Email: manitobalibraryconsortium@gmail.
com
www.umanitoba.ca/libraries/mlci

NEOS
1-01H Rutherford Library South
University of Alberta
Edmonton AB T6G 2J8
Tel: + 1 780 492 0075
Fax: + 1 780 492 5083
www.neoslibraries.ca
NEOS Manager: Anne Carr-Wiggin
Email: anne.carr-wiggin@ualberta.ca

Novanet, Inc.
1550 Bedford Hwy, #501
Bedford, Nova Scotia
Canada B4A 1E6
Tel: +1 902 453 2461
Fax: +1 902 453 2369
http://novanet.ns.ca
Manager: Bill Slauenwhite
Email: bill.slauenwhite@novanet.ns.ca

OCLC Canada
955, avenue de Catania, bureau 135,
Brossard, Québec   J4Z 3V5
Canada
Tel: +1 450 656 8955
Fax: +1 450 618 8029
Email: canada@oclc.org
www.oclc.org/ca

Ontario Council of University Libraries
(OCUL)
University of Toronto Library
130 St. George St.
Toronto, ON M5S 1A5
Canada
Tel: +1 416 946 0578
Fax: +1 416 978 6755
Executive Director: Kathy Scardellato
Email: kathy.scardellato@ocul.on.ca
www.ocul.on.ca

Réseau informatisé des bibliothèques
gouvernementales du Québec (RIBG)
Centre de services partagés du Québec
1056, rue Louis Alexandre Taschereau,
RC local 337, Québec G1R 5E6
Canada
Tel: +1 418 646 3578
Fax: +1 418 644-2284
Email: ribg@cspq.gouv.qc
www.ribg.gouv.qc.ca

Saskatchewan Multitype Database
Licensing Program (MDLP)
8-1945 Hamilton Street
Regina, Saskatchewan
Canada S4P 2C8
Tel: +1 306 787 1306
Fax: +1 306 787 2029
Email: MDLP@library.gov.sk.ca
www.lib.sk.ca/staff/dblicensing/index.html

TriUniversity Group of Libraries (TUG)
Library, Room L226
Wilfrid Laurier University
70 University Avenue West
Waterloo, Ontario N2L 3C5
Canada
Tel: +1 519 884 0710 x3673
Fax: +1 519 884 8023
www.tug-libraries.on.ca
Programme Coordinator: Ron MacKinnon
Email: rmk@uoguelph.ca
Chile

Alerta a Conocimiento (Alerta)
1550 Bedford Hwy, #501
Bedford, Nova Scotia
Av. Providencia 2040, Oficina C -
Providencia, Santiago
Chile
Tel: +56 2 233 7908
Fax: +56 2 233 9750
www.alerta.cl

China

China Academic Library and Information
System (CALIS)
CALIS Administrative Center
Room 135, Peking University Library
Peking University
HaiDian District
Beijing 100871
P.R.China
Tel: +86 10 6275 4701
Fax: +86-10 6275 4701
Email: office@calis.edu.cn
www.calis.edu.cn

Denmark

Denmark's Electronic Research Library
(DEFF)
Danish Agency for Libraries and Media
H.C. Andersens Boulevard 2
1553 Copenhagen V
Denmark
Tel: +45 33 733 373
Fax: +45 33 733 372
Email deff@bibliotekogmedier.dk
www.deff.dk

Egypt

Egyptian Universities' Library
Consortium
96 Ahmed Orabi St., engineers
12441 Giza
Egypt
Tel: +20 2 3345 8610 x115/158
Fax: +20 2 3345 8610 x158
www.eul.edu.eg

Estonia

Estonian Libraries Network Consortium
(ELNET)
Registrikood: 80013459
Tõnismägi 2
Tallinn, 10122
Estonia
Tel: +372 737 5736
Email: elnet@elnet.ee
www.elnet.ee

Finland

The National Electronic Library (of
Finland) (FinELib)
The National Library of Finland
P.O.Box 26 (Teollisuuskatu 23-25)
FIN-00014 University of Helsinki
Finland
Fax: +358 9 1914 4605
Email: finelib@helsinki.fi
www.nationallibrary.fi/libraries/finelib.html

Linnea2 Consortium
The National Library of Finland / Linnea
Database Services
P.O.B. 26 (Teollisuuskatu 23)
FIN-00014 University of Helsinki
Finland
Email: linnea-posti@helsinki.fi
www.linneanet.fi/english/index.htm

France

Consortium universitaire de publications
numériques (COUPERIN)
Maison des Universités
103 Boulevard Saint-Michel
75005 Paris
France
Tel: +33 1 69 47 89 22
Fax: +33 1 69 47 89 72
Email: emilie.barthet@couperin.org
www.couperin.org
President: Geneviève Gourdet

Germany

Bayern-Konsortium
Bayerische Staatsbibliothek
Ludwigstrasse 16
80539 Muenchen
Germany
Tel: +49 89 28638 2300
Fax: +49 89 28638 2979
www.bayern-konsortium.de

Friedrich-Althoff-Konsortium (FAK)
c/o Konrad-Zuse-Zentrum für
Informationstechnik Berlin (ZIB)
Takustr. 7, 14195 Berlin-Dahlem
Germany
Tel: +49 30 8418 5349
Tel: +49 30 8418 5269
Email: fak-office@zib.de
www.althoff-konsortium.de

Gemeinsamer Bibliotheks Verbund (GBV)
Verbundzentrale des GBV (VZG)
Platz der Göttinger Sieben 1
37073 Göttingen
Germany
Tel: +49 551 395 277
Email: diedrichs@gbv.de
www.brzn.de
Executive Director: Dipl.-Kfm. Reiner
Diedrichs

He-BIS Konsortium
Universitätsbibliothek Johann Christian
Senckenberg
Bockenheimer Landstraße 134 - 138
60325 Frankfurt am Main
Head: Sylvia Weber
Tel: +49 69 7983 9238
Fax: +49 69 7983 9538
www.hebis.de/hebis-konsortium
Contact: Sylvia Weber
Email: s.weber@ub.uni-frankfurt.de

Greece

Hellenic Academic Libraries (HEAL) Link
Aristotle University of Thessaloniki
Library of Physics and Informatics 54006
Thessaloniki
Greece
Tel: +30 2310 998210
Fax: +30 2310 999428
www.heal-link.gr
www.heal-link.gr/enh
Contact: Claudine Dervos, Steering
Commitee HEAL-Link
Email: dervos@physics.auth.gr

Hong Kong

Joint University Libraries Advisory
Committee (JULAC)
JULAC Office, Architecture Library
Chinese University of Hong Kong
6th Floor, Wong Foo Yuan Building
Hong Kong
Tel: +852 2696 1143
Fax: +852 2603 6584
www.julac.org
Project Manager: Anne Douglas Julack
Email: adouglas@cuhk.edu.hk

India

Indian National Digital Library in Engineering Science and Technology (INDEST)
Librarian, Central Library
Indian Institute of Technology Bombay
P.O. Powai, Mumbai - 400 076
India
Tel: +91 22 2572 0227/8920, 2576 8921
Fax: +91 22 2572 0227
http://paniit.iitd.ac.in/indest
National Coordinator: Dr. Jagdish Arora,
Email: jarora@admin.iitb.ac.in

Forum for Resource Sharing in Astronomy & Astrophysics (FORSA)
Indian Institute of Astrophysics,
Koramangala, Bangalore 560034
India
Tel: +91 80 2565 1384
Fax: +91 80 2565 5149
Email: sunitab@ncra.tifr.res.in
www.ncra.tifr.res.in/library/forsaweb/index.htm

UGC-Infonet E-Journals Consortium
Central Library
Information and Library Network
Navrangpura
Ahmedabad – 380009
India
Tel: + 91 79 2630 8528/4695/5971
http://web.inflibnet.ac.in/econ
Contact: Dr.Jagdish Arora Director,
INFLIBNET Consortium
Email: director@inflibnet.ac.in

Ireland

IRIS Consortium of University and Research Libraries
Room 235, James Joyce Library
Belfield, Dublin 4
Ireland
Tel: +353 1716 7533
Email: director@inflibnet.ac.in
www.irelibrary.ie/

Israel

MALMAD: Israel Center for Digital
Information Services
16 Klausner st., P.O.B. 39513
Tel Aviv 61394
Israel
Tel: +972 3 646 0551
Fax: +972 3 646 0557
Email: malmad@mail.iucc.ac.il
http://libnet.ac.il
http://malmad.iucc.ac.il

Italy

Coordinamento Interuniversitario Basi
dati & Editoria in Rete (CIBER)
Via dei Tizii 6
00185 Roma
Italy
Tel: +39 6 444 86605
Fax: +39 6 495 7083
Email: ciber-segreteria@caspur.it
http://ciber.caspur.it/

Italian National Forum on Electronic
Information Resources (INFER)
Florence
Tel: +39 55 468 5393
Fax +39 55 468 528
www.infer.it
Contact: tommaso.giordano@iue.it

Japan

Japan Association of National University
Libraries, (JANUL)
Planning and Liaison Section, General
Affairs Division
General Library, University of Tokyo Library
System
7-3-1 Hongo, Bunkyo-Ku
Tokyo, 113-0033
Japan
Tel: +81 3 5841 2612/2613
Email: kikaku@lib.u-tokyo.ac.jp
www.soc.nii.ac.jp/janul/index-e.html

Korea (Republic South)

KERIS (KERIS-LINK)
International Cooperation & Public
Relations Team, Policy Planning Office
Korea Education & Research Information
Service
22-1 KERIS Building
Ssangnim-dong, Jung-gu
Seoul 100-400
South Korea
Tel: +82 2 2118 1478
Fax: +82 2 2278 4277
Email: minkim@keris.or.kr
www.keris.or.kr

Lebanon

Lebanese Academic Library Consortium
(LALC)
C/O Miss Houeida Kammourié-Charara
Lebanese American University
Riyad Nassar Library
P.O. Box 13-5053 - Chouran
Beirut 1102 2801
Lebanon
Tel: +961 1 786 456 x1817
Fax: +961 1 867 098

Lesotho

Lesotho Library Consortium (LELICO)
Maseru
Tel: +266 22 340 468
Fax +266 22 340 000
www.lelico.org.ls
Coordinator: Dr Moshoeshoe-Chadzingwa

Lithuania

Lithuanian Research Library Consortium
(LMBA)
Gedimino pr. 51,
LT-01504 Vilnius
Lithuania
Tel.: +370 85 249 7023
Fax: +370 85 249 6129
www.lmba.lt

Luxembourg

Consortium Luxembourg
C/o National Library of Luxembourg
37 F. D. Roosevelt Boulevard
L-2450 Luxembourg
Tel: +352 260 959 412
Fax: +352 260 959 500
Project Manager: Patrick Peiffer
Email: Patrick.peiffer@bnl.etat.lu
www.portail.bnl.lu

Malawi

MALICO: Malawi Library and Information
Consortium
Kamuzu College of Nursing library
Private Bag 1, Lilongwe
Malawi
Email: malice@kcn.unima.mw
www.bunda.sdnp.org.mw/malico.htm
www.malico.mw

Mexico

**Instituto Tecnológico y de Estudios
Superior de Monterrey (ITESM)**
Biblioteca Digital
http://millenium.itesm.mx

Netherlands

SURFdiensten (SURF)
SURFdiensten bv
Onderdoor 74
3995 DX Houten
(Postbus 110 3990 DC Houten)
The Netherlands
Tel: +31 30 298 3000
Fax: +31 30 296 5851
Email admin@surfdiensten.nl
www.surfdiensten.nl

UKB: Dutch Association of University
Libraries, the Royal Library and the Library
of the Royal Dutch Academy of Science
Secretariaat UKB
Postbus 90407
2509 LK Den Haag
Tel: +31 70 314 03 68
Email: ukb@kb.nl
www.ukb.nl

New Zealand

**Electronic Purchasing in Collaboration
(EPIC)**
EPIC Manager, c/o National Library of
New Zealand, PO Box 1467
Wellington 6140
New Zealand
Tel: +64 4 4743058
Email: epic@epic.org.nz
www.epic.org.nz

Norway

Norwegian Consortium for Medical
Information
Health Library
PO Box 7004 St. Olavs plass,
0130 Oslo
Norway
Tel: +47 2325 5000
Email: redaksjonen@helsebiblioteket.no
www.helsebiblioteket.no

Norwegian Archive, Library and Museum
Authority (ABM-consortium)
ABM-utvikling
Postboks 8145 Dep
0033 OSLO
(Observatoriegata 1b, 0254 Oslo)
Norway
Tel: +47 2311 7500
Tel: +47 2311 7501
Email: post@abm-utvikling.no
www.abm-utvikling.no/prosjekter/
Bibliotek/konsortieavtaler/index.html

RBT, Norway: National Office for
Research Documentation, Academic
and Special Libraries
POB 8046 Dep
0030 Oslo
Norway
Tel: +47 2311 8900
Fax: +47 2311 8901
Email: rbt@rbt.no
www.abm-utvikling.no/prosjekter/
Bibliotek/Fagbibliotek/index.html

Poland

Poznan Foundation of Scientific
Librariesul
Powstanców Wlkp. 16
61-895 Poznan
Tel: +48 61 854 3141
Fax: +48 61 854 3149
Email: office@pfsl.poznan.pl
www.pfsl.poznan.pl

Portugal

Fundação para a Computação Ciêntifica
Nacional (FCCN)
Av. do Brasil, 101
Lisboa
Portugal
Fax: +351 21 847 2167
Email: info@b-on.pt
www.b-on.pt

Russia

National Electronic Information
Consortium of Russia (NEICON)
13/17, Big Kozlovsky per
Moscow, Russia 107078
Tel: +7 495 621 83 22
Fax: +7 495 928 18 04
Email: podpiska@neicon.ru
www.neicon.ru

ICSTI Resource Network
1b Kuusinena st., 125252,
Moscow, Russian Federation
Tel: +7 499 198 7021
Fax: +7 499 943 0089
Email: info@icsti.su
www.icsti.su

South Africa

Cape Library Cooperative (CALICO)
P O Box 18094
WYNBERG7824
Cape Town
South Africa
Tel: +27 21 763 7103/7100
Fax: +27 21 763 7117
www.adamastor.ac.za/Academic/Calico
www.calico.ac.za
Acting CALICO Director: Mrs Nikki
Crowster

Research Libraries Consortium (South
Africa) (RLC)
c/o Office of the Director
UCT Libraries
University of Cape Town
Private Bag X3
Rondebosch 7701
South Africa
Tel: +27 21 780 1432
Fax +27 21 780 1432
Email: sarah.loat@hri.ac.uk

South African National Library and
Information Consortium (SANLIC)
P O Box 11589
Centurion 0046
South Africa
Tel: + 27 12 663 8559
Fax: +27 12 643 1683
Email: sasli@SANLiC.ac.za
www.cosalc.ac.za

Gauteng and Environs Library
Consortium, South Africa (GAELIC)
P.O. Box 418
Wits, 2050
South Africa
Telefax: +27 11 717 9364
www.gaelic.ac.za

Spain

Consorci de Biblioteques
Universitaries de Catalunya (CBUC)
Gran Capità, 2-4, NEXUS Building, 3rd
floor, office 301, 08034 Barcelona
Spain
Tel: +34 93 205 6464
Fax: +34 93 205 6979
Email: info@cbuc.es
www.cbuc.es

Consorcio de Bibliotecas de Galicia
(bugalicia)
Ramón Piñeiro, 4 - Entreplanta
15702 Santiago de Compostela
Dna. Míriam Alonso Rodríguez
Spain
Tel: +34 986 813 843
Fax: +34 881 031 005
Email: comunicacion@bugalicia.es
www.bugalicia.org

Consorcio Madroño
Universidad Rey Juan Carlos
Edificio Biblioteca. Consorcio Madroño
C/ Tulipán s/n 28933 Móstoles (Madrid)
Spain
Tel: +34 91 488 7060, 609 59 0151
Fax: +34 91 488 8572
www.consorciomadrono.net

CSIC Library Network (CSIC-CBIC)
CSIC Libraries Coordination Unit
 C/ Joaquín Costa 22, 3ª planta.
28002 Madrid
Spain
Tel: +34 91 568 1663
Fax: +34 91 568 1681
Email: canton@bib.csic.es
http://bibliotecas.csic.es

Sweden

BIBSAM Sweden: Consortium of
Research Libraries
Royal Library's Department for National
Co-Operation, Box 5039
S-102 41 STOCKHOLM
Sweden
Tel: +46 8 463 4272
Fax +46 8 463 4274
Email: sasli@SANLiC.ac.za
http://www.kb.se/bibsam/english/first.htm

Switzerland

Consortium of Swiss Academic Libraries
ETH-Bibliothek
Rämistrasse 101
CH-8092 Zürich
Switzerland
Tel: +41 1 632 84 26
Fax: +41 1 632 14 30
Email: contact@consortium.ch
http://lib.consortium.ch

Informationsverbund Deutschschweiz
(IDS)
Zentralbibliothek Zürich Postfach
CH-8025 Zürich
Switzerland
Tel: +41 1 268 32 84
Email: oliver.thiele@zb.unizh.ch
www.informationsverbund.ch

Réseau des bibliothèques romandes et
tessinoises (RERO)
Library Network of Western Switzerland
Av. de la Gare 45 Av de la Gare 45
CH - 1920 Martigny
Switzerland
Tel: +41 27 721 8585
Fax: +41 27 721 8586
Email: info@rero.ch
www.rero.ch

Taiwan

Consortium on Core Electronic
Resources in Taiwan (CONCERT)
14F, 106 Sec. 2,
Hoping East Road,
Taipei
Taiwan ROC
Tel: +886 2 2737 7754
Fax: +886 2 2737 7839
Email:ir@mail.stpi.org.tw
www.stpi.org.tw

Turkey

ULAKBIM: Turkish National Academic
Site License Project (UASL)
TÜBİTAK-ULAKBİM
YÖK Binası B5 Blok
06539 Bilkent / Ankara
Turkey
Tel: +90 312 298 9200 (Santral)
Tel: +90 312 298 9302 (Müdürlük)
Fax: +90 312 298 9393
www.ulakbim.gov.tr/cabim/uasl

Ukraine

Association "Informatio-consortium"
Kiev-10, PO box 110
Kiev, 01010
Ukraine
Tel: +380 44 501 1295
Tel/Fax: +380 44 286 2443
Email: informatio.consortium@gmail.com
www.informatio.org.ua

UK

EduServe CHEST
Royal Mead, Railway Place
Bath, BA1 1SR
UK
Tel: +44 (0)1225 470523
Fax: +44 (0)1225 474301
Email: help@eduserv.org.uk
www.eduserv.org.uk

Joint Information Systems Committee
(JISC)
Brettenham House (South Entrance)
5 Lancaster Place
London WC2E 7EN
UK
Tel: +44 (0) 20 3006 6099
Fax: +44 (0) 20 7240 5377
www.jisc.ac.uk/
Collections Team Manager: Liam Earney
Tel: +44 (0) 203 006 5002
Email: l.earney@jisc.ac.uk

North-East and Yorkshire Academic
Libraries Purchasing Consortium
(NEYAL)
NEYAL Assistant
City Campus Library
Northumbria University
Newcastle upon Tyne, NE1 8ST
UK
Tel: +44 (0)191 227 4142
Email:elizabeth.beach@northumbria.ac.uk
http://neyal.procureweb.ac.uk/public/
home.htm

North West Academic Libraries (NOWAL)
Room 212
Department of Information and
Communications
Manchester Metropolitan University
Geoffrey Manton Building
Rosamond Street West, Off Oxford Road
Manchester M15 6LL
UK
Tel: +44 (0)161 247 6673
Fax: +44 (0)161 247 6846
www.nowal.ac.uk
Executive Secretary: Peter Wynne
Email: p.wynne@mmu.ac.uk

Research Councils UK Libraries and
Information Consortium (RESCOLINC)
Polaris House
North Star Avenue
Swindon SN2 1ET
UK
Tel: +44 (0) 1793 444420
Email: info@rcuk.ac.uk
www.rcuk.ac.uk/default.htm

Research Libraries UK (formerly
Consortium of University Research
Libraries)
Maughan Library and Information Services
Centre, King's College London
Chancery Lane
London WC2A 1LR
UK
Tel: +44 (0) 207 848 2137
www.rluk.ac.uk/
Acting Executive Director & Data Services
Manager (based in Birmingham office):
Dr Mike Mertens
Tel: +44 (0)121 415 8107
Email: mike.mertens@rluk.ac.uk

Scottish Confederation of University and
Research Libraries (SCURL)
National Library of Scotland
33 Salisbury Place
Edinburgh EH9 1SL
UK
Tel: +44 (0) 131 623 3940
Fax: + 44 (0) 131 623 3984
http://scurl.ac.uk
Service Development Manager: Jill Evans
Email: j.evans@nls.uk

Scottish Digital Library Consortium
(SDCL)
Main Library, University of Edinburgh
George Square, Edinburgh EH8 9LJ
UK
Tel: +44 (0) 131 651 5205
www.nls.uk/sdlc
Head, Digital Library Section: Simon
Bains
Email: simon.bains@ed.ac.uk

Society of College, National and
University Libraries (SCONUL)
102 Euston Street
London NW1 2HA
UK
Tel: +44 (0) 20 7387 0317
Fax: +44 (0) 20 7383 3197
Email: info@sconul.ac.uk
www.sconul.ac.uk

Southern Universities Purchasing
Consortium (SUPC)
University of Reading
London Road, Reading RG1 5AQ
Tel: +44 (0) 118 378 2542
Fax: +44 (0) 118 378 2404
Email: supc@reading.ac.uk
http://supc.procureweb.ac.uk

Wales Higher Education Libraries Forum
(WHELF)
National Library of Wales
Aberystwyth, Ceredigion SY23 3BU
Email: eak@aber.ac.uk
http://whelf.ac.uk

USA

Academic Business Library Directories
(ABLD)
Email: webmaster@abld.org
www.abld.org

Academic Libraries of Indiana
Chair of Resource Advisory Committee:
Kirsten A. Leonard (Indiana University,
Kokomo)
Tel: +1 765 455 9346
Email: KALeonar@iuk.edu
http://ali.bsu.edu

American International Consortium for
Academic Libraries (AMICAL)
C/o University Library
The American University of Paris
9 rue de Monttessuy
75007 Paris
France
Tel:+33 1 40 62 05 57
Fax: +33 1 45 56 92 89
http://ac.aup.fr/amical

Amigos Library Services, Inc.
14400 Midway Road
Dallas, TX 75244-3509
USA
Tel: +1 972 851 8000
Fax: +1 972 991 6061
Email: amigos@amigos.org
www.amigos.org

Arizona Health Information Network
(AZHIN)
1501 N Campbell Ave
PO Box 245079
Tucson AZ, 85724-5079
USA
Tel: +1 520 626 8087
Fax: +1 520 626 2922
Email: coordinator@azhin.org
www.azhin.org

Arizona University Libraries Consortium
(AULC)
PO Box 871006
Tempe AZ 85287-1006
USA
Tel: +1 602 965 5250
Fax +1 602 965 9169
www.statemuseum.arizona.edu/library/
cazmal

ARKLink Consortium of Arkansas
Academic Libraries
ARKLink Library Consortium, Inc.
Henry Terrill, Treasurer
Box 12267
Searcy, AR 72149
USA
http://arklink-libraries.arkansas.edu

Association of South-Eastern Research
Libraries
1438 West Peachtree Street, N.W., Suite
200
Atlanta, Georgia   30309-2955
USA
Tel: +1 404 892 0943
Fax: +1 404 892 7879
www.aserl.org
Executive Director: John Burger
Email: jburger@aserl.org

Associated Colleges of the South
1975 Century Blvd. NE Suite 10
Atlanta, GA 30345-3316
USA
Tel: +1 404 636 9533
Fax: +1 404 636 9558
Email: acs@colleges.org
www.colleges.org

Bibliographical Research Center
14394 East Evans Avenue
Aurora, CO 80014
USA
Tel: +1 303 751 6277, 800 397 1552
Email: info@bcr.org
www.bcr.org

Boston Library Consortium (BLC)
700 Boylston Street Boston
 MA 02117
USA
Tel: +1 617 262 0380
Fax: +1 617 262 0163
www.blc.org

Bowen Central Library of Appalachia
(BCLA)
626 Hills Gate Circle
Seymour TN 37865
USA
Tel: +1 865 548 5450
Fax: +1 865 577 9278
Email: tonyk@acaweb.org
www.acaweb.org/content.
aspx?sid=2&pid=35

Califa
Northern California Office
32 W. 25th Avenue, Suite 201
San Mateo, CA 94403
USA
Tel: +1 650 356 2131/572 2746
Fax: +1 650 572 2746

Southern California Office
248 E. Foothill Blvd., Suite #101
Monrovia, CA 91016
USA
Tel: +1 310 348 9578
Fax: +1 323 375 1463
Email: califa@califa.org
www.califa.org

California Digital Library (CDL)
University of California
Office of the President
415 20th Street, 4th Floor
Oakland, CA 94612-2901
USA
CDL Administration: +1 510 987 0425
Fax: + 1 510 893 5212
Email: cdl@www.cdlib.org
www.cdlib.org

California State University Systemwide
Electronic Information Resources (CSU-
SEIR)
CSU Office of the Chancellor
401 Golden Shore, 3rd Floor
Long Beach, CA 90802-4210
USA
Fax: +1 562 951 4942
www.calstate.edu/SEIR

Chesapeake Research Information
Library Alliance
www.cirla.org

Chicago Library System (CLS)
Chicago Library System
224 S. Michigan Avenue
Chicago, IL 60604
USA
Tel: +1 312 341 8500
Fax: +1 312 341 1985
www.chilibsys.org

College Center for Library Automation
(CCLA)
Chicago Library System
224 S. Michigan Avenue
Chicago, IL 60604
USA
Tel: +1 312 341 8500
Fax: +1 312 341 1985
www.cclaflorida.org

Colorado Alliance of Research Libraries
(CARL)
3801 E Florida Ave, Suite 515
Denver, CO 80210
USA
Tel: +1 303 759 3399
Fax: +1 303 759 3363
www.coalliance.org/

Colorado Library Consortium (CLiC)
7400 E. Arapahoe Road
 Ste. 105 Centennial, CO 80112
USA
Tel: +1 303 422 1150
Fax: +1 303 431 9752
www.clicweb.org

Committee on Institutional Cooperation
(CIC) Center for Library Initiatives
1819 South Neil Street, Suite D
Champaign, IL 61820-7271
USA
Tel: +1 217 333 8475
Fax: +1 217 244 7127
Email: cic@staff.cic.net
www.cic.uiuc.edu

Community College Libraries
Consortium (CCLC)
Community College League
2017 O Street, Sacramento, CA 95814
USA
Tel: + 1 951 776 9788
www.cclibraries.org
Library Consortium Director: Sarah Raley
Email: sarahraley@ccleague.org

Connecticut Library Consortium (CLC)
234 Court Street
Middletown, CT 06457-3304
USA
Tel: +1 860 344 8777
Fax: +1 860 344 9199
Email: clc@ctlibrarians.org
www.ctlibrarians.org

Consortium of Academic and Research
Libraries in Illinois (CARLI)
100 Trade Centre Drive, Suite 303
Champaign, IL 61820-7233
USA
Email: support@carli.illinois.edu
www.carli.illinois.edu
Executive Director: Susan Singleton
Tel: + 1 217 244 516 7
Email: ssingle@uillinois.edu

Cooperating Libraries in Consortium
(CLIC)
1619 Dayton Avenue
Suite 204, St Paul, MN 55104
USA
Tel: +1 651 644 3878
Fax: +1 651 644 6258
www.clic.edu
Executive Director: Tom Nichol
Email: tom.nichol@clic.edu

Co-operative Computer Services
3355 N. Arlington Heights Road
Arlington Heights, Illinois
60004-15
Tel: +1 847 342 5300
Fax: +1 847 342 8099
www.ccs.nsls.lib.il.us

The Council of Connecticut Academic
Library Directors (CCALD)
37 Pequot Avenue
New London, CT 06320
USA
Tel: + 1860 701 5155
Fax: +1 860 701 5099
http://faculty.quinnipiac.edu/ccald/ccald.
html
Director of Library Service: Suzanne M
Risley
Email: risley_s@mitchell.edu

Federal Library Information Network
(FedLink)
101 Independence Ave, SE
Washington, DC 20540-4935
USA
Tel: +1 202 707 4800
www.loc.gov/flicc/fedlink.html

Federation of Kentucky Academic
Libraries (FoKAL)
http://fokal.pbworks.com/
Library Director: John Stemmer
Tel: +1 502 452 8140
Email: jstemmer@bellarmine.edu

Fenway Library Consortium
550 Huntington Ave
Boston MA 02115
USA
Tel: +1 617 442 2384
www.fenwaylibraries.org

Florida Center for Library Automation
(FCLA)
5830 NW 39th Ave
Gainesville, Fl 32606
USA
Tel: +1 352 392 9020
http://fclaweb.fcla.edu

Georgia Library Learning Online (Galileo)
University System of Georgia
270 Washington Street, S.W.
Atlanta, GA 30334
USA
www.galileo.usg.edu

Great Western Libraries Alliance
Joni Blake, PhD
Executive Director
5109 Cherry Street
Kansas City, MO 64110
USA
Tel: +1 816 926 8765
Fax: +1 816 926 8790
Email: joni@gwla.org
www.gwla.org

Illinois Library and Information Network
(ILLINET)
Room 310, Gwendolyn Brooks Building
300 S. 2nd Street
Springfield, IL 62701-1796
USA
Tel: +1 217 785 1532
Fax: +1 217 557-2619
www.cyberdriveillinois.com/departments/
library/who_we_are/illinet.html

Georgia Online Database (GOLD)
DTAE/Office of Public Library Services
Suite 150, 1800 Century Place
Atlanta, GA 30345-4304
Tel: +1 404 982 3560
Fax:+1 404 982 3563
www.public.lib.ga.us/pls/gold
www.georgialibraries.org/lib/gold

Indiana Cooperative Library Services
Authority (INCOLSA)
6202 Morenci Trail
Indianapolis, Indiana 46268
USA
Tel: +1 317 298 6570
Fax: +1 317 328 2380
www.incolsa.net

INFOhio the Information Network for
Ohio Schools
35 E Chestnut 8th Floor
Columbus OH 43215
USA
Tel: +1 614 485 6731
Fax: +1 614 752 2940
www.infohio.org

Kansas City Metropolitan Library and
Information Network (KCMLIN)
15624 E. 24 Highway
Independence, MO64050
Tel: +1 816 521 7257
Fax; +1 816 461 0966
Email: susanburton@kcmlin.org
www.kcmlin.org

Kansas Regents Library Database
Consortium (RLDC)
Email: rldc@ku.edu
www.lib.ku.edu /rldc/index.shtml

Kentucky Virtual Library
1024 Capital Center Drive
Frankfort, KY 40601
USA
Tel: +1 877 740 4357
Fax: +1 502 573 0222
www.kyvl.org

Library of California (LOC)
P.O. Box 942837
Sacramento, CA 94237-0001
USA
Tel: +1 916 653 7532
Fax: + 1 916 653 8443
www.library.ca.gov/loc

Library and Information Resources
Network (LIRN)
7855 126th Avenue North
Largo, FL 33773
USA
Tel: +1 727 536 0214
Fax: +1 727 530 3126
Email: info@lirn.net
www.lirn.net

Loan Shark
State Library of Louisiana
P.O. Box 131
Baton Rouge LA 70821
USA
Tel: +1 225 342 4920
Fax: +1 225 219 4725
Email: vsmith@state.lib.la.us
http://la.library.net/

Long Island Library Resources Council
(LILRC)
627 N. Sunrise Service Road
Bellport, NY 11713-1540
USA
Tel: +1 631 675 1570
Fax: +1 631 675 1573
Email: director@lilrc.org
www.lilrc.org

LOUIS: The Louisiana Library Network
200 Frey Computing Services Center
Tower Dr. at S. Stadium LSU
Baton Rouge, LA
USA
Tel: +1 225 578 3700
Fax: +1 225 578 3709
Email: rjb@lsu.edu
www.louislibraries.org

Louisiana Library Connection
State Library of Louisiana
P.O. Box 131
Baton Rouge LA 70821
USA
Tel: +1 225 342 7962
Fax: +1 225 219 4725
Email: rbordelo@state.lib.la.us
http://lalibcon.state.lib.la.us

LYRASIS (merger of PALINET and
SOLINET)
Atlanta Office
Suite 200, 1438 West Peachtree
Street, NW
Atlanta, GA 30309
USA
Tel: +1 404 892 0943
Fax: +1 404 892 7879
www.lyrasis.org

Philadelphia Office
3000 Market Street, Suite 200
Philadelphia, PA 19104-2801
USA
Tel: +1 215 382 7031
Fax: +1 215 382 0022

Maine InfoNet
University of Maine
5784 York Village, Suite 58
Orono, Maine 04469-5784
USA
Fax: +1 207 581 3095
http://maineinfonet.org

Maryland Digital Library
University of Maryland
4101 McKeldin Library
College Park, MD 20742
USA
Tel: + 1 301 314 0964
http://md-diglib.org
Contact: Sue Baughman
Email: mbaughma@umd.edu

Massachusetts Board of Library
Commissioners (MBLC)
Massachusetts Board of Library
Commissioners
98 North Washington St., Suite 401
Boston, Massachusetts 02114
USA
Tel: +1 617 725 1860
Fax: +1 617 725 0140
www.mlin.lib.ma.us

Metropolitan New York Library Council
(METRO)
57 East 11th Street, 4th floor
New York, NY 10003-4605
USA
Tel: +1 212 228 2320
Fax: +1 212 228 2598
www.metro.org

Michigan Library Consortium
1407 Rensen Street, Suite 1
Lansing, MI 48910-3657
USA
Tel: +1 517 394 2420
Fax: +1 517 492 3808
http://mlc.lib.mi.us

Minitex Library Information Network
University of Minnesota
15 Andersen Library
222 21st Avenue South
Minneapolis, MN 55455-0439
USA
Tel: +1 612 624 4002
Fax: +1 612 624 4508
www.minitex.umn.edu

Minnesota Library Information Network
St. Cloud State University
310 Miller Center
720 Fourth Avenue South
St. Cloud, MN 56301-4498\
USA
Fax: +1 320 255 4778
Email: linda.conway@so.mnscu.edu
www.mnlink.org

Mississippi Alliance for Gaining New
Opportunities through Library Information
Access (MAGNOLIA)
P.O. Box 5408
Mississipi State, MS 39762
USA
Tel: +1 662 325 8542
Fax: +1 662 325 4263
Email: scunetto@library.msstate.edu
http://library.msstate.edu/magnolia

Missouri Education and Research
Libraries Information Network (MERLIN)
University of Missouri Library Systems
1001 E. Cherry, Suite 104
Columbia, MO 65201-7931
USA
Fax:+1 573 884 6023
http://merlin.missouri.edu

Missouri Library Network Corporation
(MLNC)
8045 Big Bend Blvd.
Suite 202 St. Louis, MO 63119-2714
USA
Tel: +1 314 918 7222
Fax: +1 314 918 7727
www.mlnc.org

MOBIUS: A Consortium of Missouri
Libraries
MOBIUS Consortium Office
3212A Le Mone Industrial Blvd
Columbia M0 65203
Tel: +1 573 882 7233
Fax: +1 573 884 3395
USA
http://mobius.missouri.edu

Missouri Research and Education
Network (MOREnet)
3212A LeMone Industrial Blvd
Columbia, MO 65201
USA
Tel: +1 573 884 6673
Fax: +1 573 884 6673
Email: info@more.net
www.more.net

Montana Library Network
Montana State Library
P.O. Box 201800
1515 East 6th Avenue
Helena MT 59620-1800
USA
Tel: +1 406 444 3115
http://montanalibraries.org

Nashville Area Library Alliance (NALA)
419 21st. Ave. South
Nashville, TN 37215
USA
Tel: +1 615 322 7120
Fax: +1 615 343 8279
www.library.vanderbilt.edu/nala/nala.htm

Network of Alabama Academic Libraries
(NAAL)
Alabama Commission on Higher
Education
P. O. Box 302000 Montgomery
AL 36130-2000
USA
Tel: +1 334 242 1998
Fax: +1 334 242 0268
www.ache.state.al.us/NAAL

Nevada Council of Academic Libraries
(NCAL)
C/o West Charleston Library
Las Vegas-Clark County Library District
USA
Tel: +1 702 507 3941
NCAL Executive Secretary: Robbie DeBuff
Email: rjdebuff@hotmail.com

NELINET, Inc.
153 Cordaville Rd., Ste. 200
Southborough, MA 01772
USA
Tel: +1 800 NELINET
Fax:+1 508 460 9455
www3.nelinet.net
Executive Director: Arnold Hirshen
Email: hirshon@nelinet.net

New England Law Library Consortium
(NELLCO)
55 Main St., Keene, NH 03431
USA
Tel: +1 603 357 3385
Fax: +1 603 357 2075
www.nellco.org
Executive Director: Tracy L. Thompson,
Email: tracy.thompson@nellco.org

New York State Higher Education
Initiative (NYSHEI)
c/o Nylink State University Plaza
Albany, New York 12246
USA
Tel: +1 518 443 5444
Fax: +1 518 432 4346
Email: nyshei@nyshei.org
www.nyshei.org

New York Three R's Organization
(NY3R's)
Campus Box 7111
NC State University
Raleigh NC 27695-7111
USA
Tel: +1 919 513 0451
Fax: +1 919 513 2588
Email: help@nclive.org
www.ny3rs.org

North Carolina Libraries and
Virtual Education (NCLive)
NCSU Libraries
Campus Box 7111
Raleigh, NC 27695-7111
USA
Fax: +1 919 513 2588
www.nclive.org/about.phtm

Northeast Florida Library Information
Network (NEFLIN)
2233 Park Avenue, Suite 402,
Orange Park, FL 32073-5569
USA
Tel: +1 904 278 5620
Fax: +1 904 278 5625
Email: office@neflin.org
www.neflin.org

NorthEast Research Libraries
Consortium (NERL)
130 Wall Street
PO Box 208240
New Haven, CT 06520
USA
Tel: +1 203 432 1764
Fax: +1 203 432 7231
Email: nerl@yale.edu
www.library.yale.edu/NERLpublic/

Nylink
State University of New York
22 Corporate Woods, 3rd Fl
Albany, NY 12211
USA
Tel: +1 518 443 5444
Fax: +1 518 432 4346
Email: help@nclive.org
http://nylink.suny.edu

Ohio Library and Information Network
(OhioLINK)
8th Floor
35 E. Chestnut Street
Columbus, OH 43215-2541
USA
Fax: +1 614 228 1807
Email: info@ohiolink.edu
www.ohiolink.edu

Ohio Public Library Information Network
(OPLIN)
2323 W. 5th Avenue, Suite 130
Columbus, Ohio 43204
Tel: +1 614 728 5252
Fax: + 1614 728 5256
Email: support@oplin.org
www.oplin.lib.oh.us

OHIONET
1500 West Lane Ave.
Columbus, OH 43221-3975
USA
Tel: +1 614 486 2966
Fax: +1 614 486 1527
www.ohionet.org

ORBIS Cascade Alliance
Orbis Cascade Alliance
1299 University of Oregon
Eugene, OR 97403-1299
USA
Fax: +1 541 3461968
Email: orbiscas@uoregon.edu
www.orbiscascade.org

Pennsylvania Academic Library
Consortium, Inc. (PALCI)
Room 333, &500 Thomas Blvd
Pittsburgh PA 15260
USA
Tel: +1 412 422 2151
Fax: +1 412 244 7537
www.palci.org
Executive Director: Dan Iddings
Email: iddings@pitt.edu

PALINET and Union Library Catalogue of
Pennsylvania (See LYRASIS)

Partnership Among South Carolina
Academic Libraries (PASCAL)
1333 Main Street, Suite 305
Columbia, South Carolina 29201
USA
Tel: +1 803 734 0900
Fax: +1 803 734 0901
http://pascalsc.org

Private Academic Library Network of
Indiana (PALNI)
6202 Morenci Trail
Indianapolis, IN 46268
USA
Tel: +1 317 298 6570
Fax: +1 317 328 2382
www.palni.edu

South Central Academic Medical
Libraries Consortium (SCAMeL)
University of North Texas Health Science
Center, Gibson D. Lewis Library
3500 Camp Bowie Boulevard
Fort Worth, Texas 76107
USA
Tel: +1 817 735 2380
Fax: +1 817 735 5158
Email: bcarter@hsc.unt.edu
www.tulane.edu/~scamel/default.htm

Southeast Florida Library Information
Network (SEFLIN)
Office 452
S.E. Wimberly Library
Florida Atlantic University
777 Glades Road
Boca Raton, FL 33431
USA
Tel: +1 877 733 5460
Fax: +1 561 208 0995
www.seflin.org

South-Eastern Library Network
(SOLINET) (See LYRASIS)

Southwestern Ohio Council for Higher
Education (SOCHE)
Miami Valley Research Park
3155 Research Blvd., Suite 204
Dayton, OH 45420-4015
Tel: +1 937 258 8890
Fax: +1 937 258 8899
Email: soche@soche.org
www.soche.org

State Assisted Academic Library Council
of Kentucky (SAALCK)
1748 Greatwood Drive Florence
KY 41042
USA
www.saalck.org
Executive Director: Anne Abate
Email: anne@saalck.org

Statewide California Electronic Library
Consortium (SCELC)
5600 Mulholland Drive, Taper 101
Los Angeles CA 90077-1519
USA
Tel: +1 310 728 6791
Fax: +1 310 471 0123
http://scelc.org

Southeastern Wisconsin Information
Technology Exchange (SWITCH)
6801 North Yates Road
Milwaukee, Wisconsin 53217
USA
Tel: +1 414 351 2423
http://caspian.switchinc.org

SUNYConnect
Office of Library & Information Services
SUNY Plaza
Albany, New York 12246
Tel: +1 518 443 5577
Fax: +1 518 443 5358
www.sunyconnect.suny.edu

SWON Libraries
South West Ohio and Neighboring
Libraries
Suite 200, 10815 Indeco Drive
Cincinnati, OH 45241-2926
USA
Tel: +1 513 751 4422
Fax: +1 513 751 0463
Email: info@swonlibraries.org
www.swonlibraries.org

Tampa Bay Library Consortium
1202 Tech Blvd., Suite 202
Tampa, FL 33619
USA
Tel: +1 813 622 8252
Fax: +1 813 628 4425
www.tblc.org

TENN-Share
P. O. Box 121924
Nashville, TN 37212
USA
Tel: +1 615 297 8393
www.tenn-share.org

Tennessee Electronic Library (TEL)
Sue Maszaros
Special Projects Coordinator
Tennessee State Library and Archives
403 7th Avenue North
Nashville, TN 37243
USA
Tel: +1 615 532 4627
Email: tsla@tn.gov
www.tntel.info
Special Projects Coordinator: Sue
Maszaros

Texas State Library and Archives
Commission
1201 Brazos
PO Box 12927
Austin TX 78711-2927
USA
Tel: +1 512 463 5455
Email: info@tsl.state.tx.us
www.texshare.edu

University of North Carolina System
(ULAC)
910 Raleigh Road, P.O. Box 2688
Chapel Hill, N.C. 27515-2688
USA
Tel: +1 919 962 4613
Email: hes@ga.unc.edu
www.northcarolina.edu/academics/ulac/
index.htm

University of Texas System Digital
Library
UTSDL Website and Resource Support
Digital Library Services Division
The General Libraries
University of Texas at Austin
PO Box P, Austin, TX 78713-7330
USA
Tel: +1 512 495 4350
Fax: +1 512 495 4347
www.lib.utsystem.edu

University System of Maryland and
Affiliated Institutions (USMAI)
University of Maryland Libraries
McKeldin Library
College Park, MD 20742-7011
USA
Tel: +1 301 405 9299
Fax: +1 301 314 9971
www.itd.umd.edu
Program Director & Director for Technical
Services: Carlen Ruschoff
Email: ruschoff@umd.edu

Utah Academic Library Consortium
(UALC)
Marriott Library, University of Utah
Salt Lake City, UT 84112-0860
USA
Tel: +1 801 581 3852
Fax + 1 801 581 3852
Email: UALCMail@library.utah.edu
www.ualc.net

Virtual Academic Library of New Jersey
(VALE)
William Paterson University
David & Lorraine Cheng Library
300 Pompton Road
Wayne NJ 07470-2103
USA
Tel: +1 973 720 3179
Fax: +1 973 720 3171
www.valenj.org

Virtual Library of Virginia (VIVA)
4400 University Drive
George Mason University
Fairfax, VA 22030-4444
USA
Tel: +1 703 993 4652
Fax: +1 703 993 4662
www.vivalib.org

Washington Research Library
Consortium (WRLC)
901 Commerce Drive
Upper Marlboro, MD 20774
USA
Tel: + 1 301 390 2000
www.wrlc.org

Washington State Libraries Statewide
Database Licensing Project
Washington State Library
PO Box 42460, Olympia, WA 98504-2460
USA
Tel: + 1 360 704 5217
Fax: +1 360 586 7575
www.secstate.wa.gov/library/libraries/
projects/sdl/?
Project Manager: Will Stuivenga
Email: wstuivenga@secstate.wa.gov

Washington State Cooperative Library
Project
Washington State Library
6880 Capitol Blvd SE - MS:42460
Olympia, WA 98504-2460
USA
Tel: +1 360 570 5587
Fax: +1 360 586 7575
http://cascade.lib.washington.edu/
screens/wclpoverview.html

West Virginia Digital Library (WVDL)
P. O. Box 5476
Charleston, WV 25361
USA
Tel: +1 304 696 2318
Fax: +1 304 696 3229
www.wvdl.org

Wisconsin Library Services (WiLS)
728 State Street, Rooms 464 and B106B
Madison, WI 53706
USA
Tel: +1 608 265 4167
Fax: +1 608 262 6067
Email: wilsill@wils.wisc.edu
www.wils.wisc.edu/International

International

Alliance for Innovation in Science and
Technology Information (AISTI)
Tel: +1 888 901 4144
Fax:+1 888 555 4444
Email: info@aisti.org
www.aisti.org

EIFL
c/o SURFfoundation
Building D, Hojel City Center
Gr. v Roggenweg 340
3531 AH Utrecht
The Netherlands
Email: info@eifl.net
www.eifl.net
Director: Rima Kupryte

Food and Agriculture Association (FAO)
Viale delle Terme di Caracalla
00153 Rome
Italy
Tel: +39 06 57051
Fax: +39 06 5705 3152
Email: FAO-HQ@fao.org
www.fao.org

International Atomic Energy Agency
(IAEA)
P.O. Box 100
Wagramer Strasse 5, A-1400 Vienna
Austria
Tel: +43 1 2600-0
Fax: +43 1 2600-7
Email: Official.Mail@iaea.org
www.iaea.org

International Coalition of Library
Consortia
OhioLINK, Suite 300,
2455 North Star Road
Columbus, OH 43221
USA
Tel: +1 614 728 3600, x322
www.library.yale.edu/consortia
Executive Director: Tom Sanville
Email: tom@ohiolink.edu

International Fund for Agricultural
Development (IFAD)
Via Paolo di Dono, 44
00142 Rome
Italy
Tel: +39 065 4591
Fax: +39 065 043 463
Email: ifad@ifad.org
www.ifad.org/

International Labour Office (ILO)
4 route des Morillons
CH-1211 Genève 22
Switzerland
Tel: +41 22 799 6111
Fax: +41 22 798 8685
Email: ilo@ilo.org
www.ilo.org

International Maritime Office (IMO)
4 Albert Embankment
London SE1 7SR
Tel: +44 (0) 20 7735 7611
Fax: +44 (0) 20 7587 3210
Email: info@imo.org
http://www.imo.org

International Telecommunications Union
(ITU)
Place des Nations
1211 Geneva 20
Switzerland
Tel: +41 22 730 5111
Fax: +41 22 733 7256
Email: itumail@itu.int
www.itu.int/net

Office of Communication of
Humanitarian Affairs (OCHA)
United Nations Secretariat, New
York, NY 10017, USA
Tel: +1 212 963 1234
Fax: +1 212 963 1013
Email:ochany@un.org
http://ochaonline.un.org/

Office of the High Commissioner for
Human Rights (OHCHR)
United Nations Secretariat, New
York, NY 10017
USA
Tel: +1 212 963 1234
Fax: +1 212 963 1013
Email: ochany@un.org
http://ochaonline.un.org

Organisation for Economic Co-operation
and Development (OECD)
OECD
2, rue André Pascal
75775 Paris Cedex 16
France
Tel.: +33 1 4524 8200
Fax: +33 1 4524 8500
www.oecd.org

United Nations System Consortium
United Nations, Dag Hammarskjold
Library
Room L-166A
New York, New York 10017
USA
Tel: +1 212 963 5142
Fax: +1 212 963 5142
www.un.org

World Bank
1818 H Street, NW
Washington, DC 20433
USA
Tel: +1 202 473 1000
Fax: +1 202 477 6391
www.worldbank.org

3.3 Contact details of the companies listed in Part One

LibreDigital
Name of Platform and website address:
Libre Digital. www.libredigital.com
Contact details:
Steve Schatz, Vice President Global Sales
Libre Digital Inc.
Headquarters
Suite 150,1835-B Kramer Lane
Austin, TX 78758
USA
Tel: +1 512 334 5102
Fax: +1 512 334 5199
Email: sschatz@libredigital.com

(UK)
John Hales
LibreDigital Ltd.
18 Soho Square
London W1D3QL
Tel: +44 (0) 207 268 3868
Fax: +44 (0) 207 025 8100
Email: JHale@libredigital.com

Aptara
Name of Platform and website address;
Aptaracorp. www.apraracorp.com
Contact details:
Chris McKeown
2 Selwyn Close
Newmarket. Suffolk, CB8 8DD
UK
Tel: +44 (0) 1638 603787
Fax: +44 (0) 7985 743589
Email: Chris.mckeown@aptaracorp.com

Atypon
Name of platform and website address:
Literatum, www.atypon.com The Atypon
Premium customers each have their own
domain and website. The Atypon Link
customers are all sharing www.atypon-
link.com
Contact details:
Nash Pal
2 Hitching Court, Blacklands Way
Abingdon OX14 1RG
UK
Tel.: +44 (0) 8703 502032
Fax: +44 (0) 1235 557986
Email: npal@atypon.com

books24x7
Name of platform and website address
Books24x7. www.books24x7.com
Contact details:
Pam Boiros
VP, Strategic Business Development
Books24x7, Inc
100 River Ridge Dr.
Norwood, MA 02062
USA
Tel: +1 781 440 0550
Fax: +1 781 440 0560
Email: pboiros@books24x7.com

Bowker

Name of platform and website address
Bowker. www.bowker.co.uk
Contact details:
Jack Tipping
Bowker (UK) Limited
1st Floor Medway House
Cantelupe Road, East Grinstead
West Sussex RH19 3BJ
UK
Tel: +44 (0) 1342 310485
Fax: +44 (0) 1342 310465
Mobile: 07854 289247
Email: jack.tipping@bowker.co.uk

codeMantra

Name of platform and website address:
codeMantra, www.codemantra.com
Contact details:
Code Mantra
Innovation House, Mill Street
Oxford, OX2 0JX
UK
Tel: + 44 (0) 1865 596723
Fax: + 44 (0) 1908 488001
Email: euroinfo@codemantra.com

Copyright Licensing Agency

Name of platform and website address:
CLA. www.cla.co.uk
Contact details:
Kevin Fitzgerald, Chief Executive
Copyright Licensing Agency
Saffron House, 6-10 Kirby Street
London EC1N 8TS
UK
Tel: +44 (0) 20 7400 3100
Fax: +44 (0) 20 7400 3101
Email: kevin.fitzgerald@cla.co.uk

Content Data Solutions

(Formerly Thomas Technology Solutions
(UK) Ltd)
Name of platform and website address
Content Data Solutions.
www.contentdsi.com
Contact details:
Content Data Solutions Inc
One Progress Drive
Horsham PA 19044-8014
USA
Tel/Fax: +1 215 682 5200

CourseSmart

Name of platform and website address:
CourseSmart. www.coursesmart.com
Contact details:
Sean Devine
Chief Executive
CourseSmart
Suite 545, 901 Mariners Island Blvd
San Mateo, CA 94404
USA
Email: Sean.devine@coursesmart.com

CrossRef

Name of platform and website address
CrossRef. www.crossref.org
Contact details:
Amy Brand
CrossRef
40 Salem Street
Lynnfield, MA 01940
USA
Tel: +1 781 295 0072
Fax: +1 781 295 0077
Email: abrand@crossref.org

UK office
Ed Pentz
Executive Director
CrossRef
3rd Floor, 130 High St
Oxford OX1 4DH
UK
Email: epentz@crossref.org

Dawsonera
Name of platform and website address
Dawsonera. www.dawsonera.com
Contact details:
Mark Howard
eContent Manager
Dawson Books
Foxhills House
Rushden NN10 6DB
UK
Tel: +44 (0)1933 417500
Fax: +44 (0)1933 417501
Mobile: 07789950721
Email: mark.howard@dawsonbooks.co.uk

ebooks.com/EBL
Name of platform and website address
Ebooks.com / EBL. www.ebooks.com
Contact details:
Suzanne Cole
Ebooks Corporation Limited
62 Bayview Terrace
Claremont WA 6010
Australia
Tel: +61 8 9385 5022
Fax: +61 8 9385 5755
Email: Suzanne@ebooks.com

EBSCO MetaPress
Name of platform and website address
MetaPress. www.metapress.com
Contact details:
Michael J. Margotta
Director, Sales and Marketing
5724 Highway 280 East
Birmingham, AL 35242-6818
USA
Tel: +1-205 991 1176
Fax: +1 205 980 3878
Email: mmargotta@metapress.com

ebrary
Name of platform and website address
ebrary OnDemand™. www.ebrary.com
Contact details:
318 Cambridge Avenue
Palo Alto
CA 94306
USA
Tel: +1 650 475 8700
Fax: +1 650 475 8881

Espresso
Name of platform and website address:
On Demand Books.
www.ondemandbooks.com
Contact details:
Dane Neller
On Demand Books
584 Broadway, Suite 1100
New York, NY 10012
USA
Tel: +1 212 966 2222
Fax: +1 212 966 2229
Email: dane@ondemandbooks.com

The European Library

Name of platform and website address:
The European Library (TEL).
http://search.theeuropeanlibrary.org/
portal/en/index.html
Contact details:
Louise Edwards
Director, The European Library
The National Library of the Netherlands
PO Box 90407, 2509 The Hague
The Netherlands
Email: louise.edwards@theeuropeanlibrary.
org

Gardners

Name of Platform and website address:
Gardners Books. www.gardners.com
Contact details:
Bob Kelly
Gardners Books, 1 Whittle Drive
Eastbourne, East Sussex BN23 6QH
UK
Tel: + 44 (0)1323 521777
Fax: +44 (0)1323 521666
Email: Bob.kelly@gardners.com

How to Moodle

Name of platform and website address:
How to Moodle. www.howtomoodle.com
Contact details:
Ray Lawrence
HowToMoodle Ltd
1 Sekforde Street
London, EC1R 0BE
UK
Tel: +44 (0) 845 226 1073
Fax: +44 (0) 7977 448886
Email: ray@howtomoodle.com

Ingenta

Name of platform and website address:
IngentaConnect. www.ingentaconnect.
com
Contact details:
Louise Tutton
Unipart House, Garsington Road
Oxford OX4 2GQ
UK
Tel: +44 (0)1865 397800
Fax: +44 (0) 1865 397801
Email: Louise.tutton@ingenta.com

Ingram Content Companies

Name of platform and website address:
Ingram Content Group.
www.ingramcontent.com
Contact details:
Ingram Content Group Inc.
1 Ingram Blvd.
La Vergne, TN 37086
USA
Email: inquiry@ingramcontent.com

Klopotek

Name of platform and website address:
Klopotek. www.klopotek.de
Contact details:
Klopotek UK Ltd
90 Long Acre, Covent Garden
London WC2E 9RZ
UK
Tel : +44 (0) 20 7716 5500
Fax: +44 (0) 20 7716 5595
www.klopotek.co.uk

Knovel

Name of platform and website address:
Knovel. www.knovel.com

Contact details:
Monica Nogueira
Director of Channel Development
Professional Societies Relations
Knovel
6664 Wilkins Avenue
Pittsburgh, PA 15217
USA
Tel: +1 866 324 5163
Email: mnogueira@knovel.com

International DOI Foundation

Dr Norman Paskin
Tel: +44 (0) 1865 559070
Email: n.paskin@doi.org
www.doi.org

Lightning Source

Name of platform and website address:
Lightning Source Inc.
www.lightningsource.com

Contact details:
David Taylor
President
Lightning Source Inc.
1246 Heil Quaker Blvd.
La Vergne, TN 37086
USA
Tel: +1 615 213 5815
Fax: +1 615 213 4725
Email: david.taylor@lightningsource.com

UK
Suzanne Wilson-Higgins
Commercial Director
Lightning Source UK
Chapter House, Pitfield, Kiln Farm
Milton Keynes, MK11 3LW
UK
Tel: +44 (0) 845 121 4567
Fax: +44 (0) 845 121 4594
Email: suzanne.wilson-higgins@
lightningsource.com

Macmillan Publishing Solutions (MPS)

Name of platform and website address:
MPS.
www.macmillanpublishingsolutions.com

Contact details:
David Robertson
Macmillan Publishing Solutions
4 Crinan Street, London N1 9XW
UK
Tel: + 44 (0) 207 843 4861
Fax: +44 (0) 207 843 4865
Email: d.robertson@macmillan.co.uk

Mark Logic

Name of platform and website address:
Mark Logic. www.marklogic.com

Contact details:
Emerson Samuels
Mark Logic Corporation
3000 Hillswood Drive
Hillswood Business Park
Chertsey, Surrey KT16 ORS
UK
Tel: + 44 (0) 2084 010 920
Fax: +44 (0) 7831 560 878
Email: Emerson.samuels@marklogic.com

mEDRA

Name of Platford and website address:
mEDRA. www.medra.org/
c/o AIE - Italian Publishers Association
Corso di Porta Romana, 108
20122 Milano
Italy
Tel: +39 2 89280803
Fax: +39 2 89280863
www.aie.it

MyiLibrary

Name of platform and website address:
MyiLibrary. www.myilibrary.com
Contact details:
Andy Alferovs
Group Sales Director
MyiLibrary Ltd
Headlands Business Park, Ringwood
Hants BH 24 3PB
Tel: +44 (0) 1202 753230
Fax: +44 (0) 1202 753298
Email: aalferovs@myilibrary.com

NetLibrary

Name of platform and website address:
NetLibary. www.netlibrary.com
Contact details:
Suzanne Kemperman
Director Public Relations
NetLibrary
Suite 103, 4888 Pearl East Circle
Boulder, Colorado, 80301
USA
Tel: +1 303 415 2548
Email: kempers@oclc.org

Nielsen BookData

Name of platform and website address:
Nielsen BookData.
www.nielsenbook.co.uk
Contact details:
Julian Sowa
The Nielsen Company
3rd Floor Midas House
62 Goldsworth Road, Woking
Surrey GU21 6LQ
UK
Tel: +44 (0) 1483 712 330
Fax: +44 (0) 1483 712 201
(ISBN, ISTC & SAN agencies):
Tel: +44 (0)870 777 8712
Email: Julian.Sowa@nielsen.com

North Plains

Name of platform and website address:
North Plains. www.northplains.com
Contact details:
Northplains
4th Floor, 510 Front Street West
Toronto, ON M5V 3H3
Canada
Tel: +1 416 345 1900
Fax: +1 416 599 0808
Email: ekallus@northplains.com

Numilog

Name of platform and website address:
Numilog. www.numilog.com
Contact details:
Dennis Zwirn
President
Numilog
113, rue Jean-Marin Naudin
92220 Bagneux
France
Tel: +33 1 45361880
Fax: +33 1 4536 1888
Email: mailto:dzwirn@numilog.com

OverDrive

Name of platform and website address:
OverDrive has the following digital platforms
and addresses:

MIDAS Technology (Retail e-bookstore
Platform for direct to consumer e-book and
digital audiobook sales, e-commerce and
digital rights management):
www.overdrive.com/midas

Digital Library Reserve (download lending
platform for e-books, audiobooks, music and
digital video)
www.dlrinc.com

Content Reserve (e-book wholesale
distribution service for publishers and online
retailers with support for multiple formats and
DRM)
www.contentreserve.com

Private Reserve (DRM fulfilment
service for publishers and institutions
for protected e-book and digital media
fulfilment through their existing websites
and portals)
www.privatereserve.com

Contact details:
Steve Potash, CEO
OverDrive Inc.
8555 Sweet Valley Drive Suite C
Cleveland, Ohio 44125 USA
Tel: +1 216 573 6886 x201
Email: spotash@overdrive.com

ProQuest

Name of platform and website address:
ProQuest's primary web platform is
Literature Online - http://lion.chadwyck.
co.uk/
Contact details:
Hugh Tomlinson
ProQuest Information & Learning
The Quorum, Barnwell Road
Cambridge CB5 8SW
UK
Tel: + 44 (0) 1223 271260
Email: hugh.tomlinson@proquest.co.uk

Safari

Name of platform and website address:
Safari Books Online.
www.safaribooksonline.com
Contact details:
Safari
1003 Gravenstein Highway North
Sebastopol, CA 95472
USA
Tel: +1 707 827 4100

Semantico

Name of platform and website address:
Semantico. www.semantico.com
Contact details:
Semantico Limited
Lees House, 21-23 Dyke Road
Brighton BN1 3FE
East Sussex
UK
Tel: +44 (0) 1273 722222
Fax: +44 (0) 1273 723232

Siemens

Name of platform and website address:
Siemens. www.siemens.com
Contact details:
Chris Lawrence, Principal Consultant
Tel: +44 (0)7740 631772
Email: chrislawrence@siemens.com
Benn Linfield, Lead Consultant
Email: benn.linfield@siemens.com
Siemens
Stadium House, 68 Wood Lane
London W12 7TA
UK

SPi-Tech

Name of platform and website address:
SPI Technologies. www.SPItech.ca
Contact details:
Suite 309, 1755 Woodward Drive,
Ottawa, Ontario K2C 0P9
Canada
Tel: +1 613 723 7741
Fax: +1 613 723 7741
Email: info@SPItech.ca

Value Chain

Name of platform and website address:
Value Chain. www.value-chain.biz/VCIL.
htm
Contact details:
Neelesh Marik
Senior Vice President &
Business Head Publishing
1 Cornhil, London EC3V 3ND
UK
Tel: +44 (0) 207 410 7390
Fax: +44 (0) 207 743 6001
Email: sales@value-chain.biz
Email: eneelesh.marik@value-chain.biz

VirtuSales

Name of platform and website address:
VirtuSales. www.virtusales.com
Contact details:
Phil Turner
Virtusales
Hove Technology Centre
St. Joseph's Close
Brighton & Hove BN3 7ES
UK
Tel: +44 (0) 1273 715630
Email: phil@virtusales.com

Vital Source

Name of platform and website address
Vital Source. http://www.vitalsource.com
Contact details:
Matt Harris
Vital Source
Suite 300, 234 Fayetteville Street
Raleigh, NC 27601
USA
Tel: 1 (800) 610 5382
Email: mmharris@vitalsource.com

3.4　Refresher on Digital Printing

There are two basic types of on-demand book: books that have been digitally printed by the publisher in anticipation of demand, but in a much shorter print run than for traditional offset litho (sometimes called 'ultra-short-run' printing); and books that are actually printed to order.

3.4.1　Ultra-short-run printing

What most customers　and some booksellers don't realise is that approximately 20 per cent of the books on the shelves of the average bookshop have been digitally printed – most books that are likely to sell fewer than 2,000 copies fall into this category. We are living in a transitional period between offset litho and digital printing. Until recently, the quality of offset printing was considered to be superior to digital printing. However, this is changing fast, and many digitally-produced books are now of a quality indistinguishable from offset litho.

Offset lithography works on the principle that ink and water don't mix. Images and text from the document are transferred to plates, which are then inked. When the plates are exposed to light, a chemical reaction occurs that allows an ink-receptive coating to be activated, resulting in a transfer of the image from the negative to the plate. The plates are the most expensive component of the offset litho process, made even more expensive by the fact that each of the four primary colours (black, cyan, magenta and yellow) must be on a separate plate). The paper is fed through the machine as one giant roll, then cut to size after printing. Costs are kept down by using the plates as much as possible once they are set up, which means producing many copies of the book at the same time.

In digital printing, commonly called Print on Demand, the book is stored in digital format. Copies can be printed in any quantity from 1 upwards. Most Print on Demand printers are 'electrographic' – laser printers that fuse toner on to paper. At the top end of the market, the printers used by companies like Lightning Source, the UK's leading POD company, are very sophisticated indeed. The books are also printed on giant rolls of paper, but different titles with different pages sizes can be printed at thesame time. Each book costs exactly the same to produce, whether one copy or five hundred copies have been printed. Obviously there becomes a point when the digitally-produced book costs more to produce than the traditionally-produced book, because of the economies of scale that can be achieved by the latter.

Whether publishers choose offset litho or Print on Demand technology therefore depends in part on how many copies of the book they want to produce. However, some publishers now realise that even if they are certain that they can sell, say, 3,000 copies of a book over a period of two years, it might still be cheaper to produce it digitally once the warehouse costs and the amount of capital tied up in stock required by traditional printing are taken into account. Digital printing also takes the pain out of editors' per-title sales projections.

3.4.2   Print to Order

Printing to order comes closer to the concept of 'true' on demand printing. From the bookseller's point of view, it is also a little trickier, because lead-times can be variable. Often the problem is not so much caused by tardiness on the part of the Print on Demand company, as by delays in the chain of communication. Most 'true' on demand books are sold via wholesalers. If the wholesaler actually has the book in stock, it will be delivered to the bookshop within 24 hours. If the book has still to be manufactured, the wholesaler should still report it 'in stock' – because no digitally-available book is technically out of print – and show a 48-hour lead-time (in the case of Lightning Source). However, the wholesalers' systems have often not been fully-updated, and not all POD companies offer the same lead-times. Sometimes the lead- time is reported as three weeks, which puts both booksellers and their customers off. It is an issue which the industry needs to address.

At present, all of the digital printers are supplying publishers, who send their orders via EDI. There is a vigorous debate taking place about the most economical way of getting the orders to the retailer. Publishers often consolidate large orders at their distribution centres. If the order is a large one, this saves money on freight, but of course means that the books are not sent to the bookseller in the shortest possible time. Statistics gathered by publishers suggest that 25 per cent of their POD commitment is for single copy orders. One option would be for them to consolidate POD and non-POD consignments and send them out at once. If ten different shops have ordered a single book, and Lightning Source is the supplier, the cheapest and quickest way would be for the publishers to drop ship via Lightning Source. Other POD companies – for example Antony Rowe and BookSurge – operate similar but slightly different models.

Lightning Source UK Ltd.
Milton Keynes UK
20 September 2010

160125UK00001B/12/P